TALK STRAIGHT
DAMMIT

How to turn negative, limiting beliefs into powerful actions to create a life of BLISS you want and deserve.

Stephen & Sonji Millet

Foreword written by Lisa Nichols

Published by: Dreamstarters Publishing
https://www.dreamstartersuniversity.com/

DREAMSTARTERS

Edited by: Andrea McCurry

DEDICATION

To Ohin, Olivia Grace, Victoria, Olivia Uvon, and
Alexandria: We dedicate this book to you, so that it may
continue to help you live a life of abundance and BLISS.

Special thanks to our parents, family and friends. We
are who we are today because you have contributed to
our lives.

CONTENTS

FOREWORD

By Lisa Nichols

So many times in my formative years I wish I had the guidelines to managing my self-talk. Little did I know, my life was a physical manifestation of the conversation going on in my head. That's huge. When I finally got that I can navigate my life's experience by first navigating the conversation going on in my head, I felt like there was an epiphany. I felt like there was an awakening. I remember the day. I was 25 years old in Spokane, Washington, reading a great book. In this book, I began to see that my thoughts were actually navigating my life experience. That was the beginning of the Lisa Nichols that you see today.

So, when that my good friends Stephen and Sonji said that they were writing a book called TALK STRAIGHT DAMMIT... Oh! The title alone captivated me! A disruptive title that says, "Give me the truth, the whole truth, and nothing but the truth. Allow me to make my decisions that shape my future based upon facts not fiction." I was super excited. Then to have the opportunity to write the forward to the book was even more exciting!

When you look at TALK STRAIGHT DAMMIT, it helps us to navigate the path of turning a negative limiting belief into a powerful conversation, that will not only influence our actions but help to create a blissful life that each one of us, you and I, actually want and we deserve. It's your birthright to live in BLISS. Most of us live in normal, we even live in chaos, and every now and again we visit BLISS. Well, TALK STRAIGHT DAMMIT teaches you how to not visit BLISS but to reside and take out real estate in the space called BLISS. No longer look through the window at other people enjoying their lives and enjoying their experiences, but now have it yourself.

Stephen breaks down so many great points as he does so masterfully as an orator, as a minister, and as a teacher. He infuses his colorful language, the ability to not only speak to a story but to show you that story. Sonji brings in her masterful, strategic, linear thinking of structure and layout to get us from 'A' to 'B' and ultimately to 'Z,' which is where we all want to end up, in a place, in that destiny that we call joy.

What I love about this book is that it allows you to identify, create, and navigate a powerful conversation, not only about yourself, but about your family, your career, your relationships, your spirituality, and your money. This book unapologetically says, who you are is so valuable that you can only give yourself the straightest, clearest, most powerful conversation about the man or woman you are becoming.

I love the definition they offer for BLISS. BLISS is the freedom to love and be loved in abundance with complete forgiveness and without judgment. This book navigates you through living in a judgment-free, forgiveness-based relationship with yourself. It is not only a must-have for you, but it is a must-have for those that you love.

Lisa Nichols

INTRODUCTION

Stephen

We are the accumulation of the total of our words, thoughts, and beliefs. What are you telling yourself about your past, present, and future? What have others told you about yourself? Many years ago, I went to a spiritual warfare conference. The entire meeting boiled down to, "Who told you that?" If you can identify the source of the information, you can choose the path you take. Sounds simple? It is. But simple doesn't mean easy. It will take time to analyze and adjust what you have programmed yourself to say, think, and believe, internally and externally about you.

You are the way you are because you practiced it. You spoke words to yourself every day that reminded you of who you are and who you believe you are. You heard others speak to you in a way that reminded you of who you are. If you heard every day, "You are beautiful," then you believed that you were beautiful. You dressed beautifully; you bought things to make you feel more beautiful. If you heard every day that you were stupid, then you believed that you were stupid. You gave up when things became difficult. Why try? You knew you were stupid. If someone told you that you were smart, you rejected it or said, "No way. I'm not smart." Repeating positive and negative statements like these is how we program or wire our lives.

We all like to think that we make up our own minds. However, many of our thoughts are set on auto-pilot, and we don't recognize that we are not in control. To create the life we want, we give away our power to those thoughts that were created earlier in our lives, often by someone else.

In this book, we are going to show you how your thoughts and beliefs affect your day-to-day life, and how you can deprogram yourself from the negative thoughts and start to reinforce the positive in your life. As you walk through the chapters, you will begin to awaken to your most powerful self that will love and be loved. This positive reinforcement starts with the conversation you have in your head. We want you to TALK STRAIGHT! Start telling yourself words that will create the life you have always desired a life of BLISS. *TALK STRAIGHT*

DAMMIT will help you to take back what you gave away because you followed those negative thoughts inside your head. Don't beat yourself up about the past or blame other people. Start today to reprogram your thoughts and therefore, your success.

We are Stephen and Sonji Millet. We are a successful couple that continues to create a life of BLISS that we live every day. I am an ordained Minister and have been a technical instructor and a comedian over the course of my life. Sonji worked in the professional sector for over 25 years as an instructor and coach. Together we have helped thousands of people become a better version of themselves.

Our life and marriage are a testimony to the wisdom we share in this book. We have written this book together to give you a husband and wife perspective. Before each section, you will find the sub-title **Stephen** or **Sonji**, depending on who wrote the section. Throughout the book, we added personal stories to provide examples where we learned the lessons we shared in this book.

"TALK STRAIGHT DAMMIT" is what we say to each other to give a gentle reminder when what we are communicating is not in alignment with our dreams. If somehow, I said something negative, then my wife would declare to me nicely, "TALK STRAIGHT DAMMIT!" Then we could both laugh and figure out how to convey the same message in a positive way.

We have read a lot of self-help and inspirational books together, and all of them give the same information in a variety of ways. We have simplified our lifetime of reading into an effortless process that is easy to understand and implement. In business, experts tell us that how we talk to others matters. But what they don't understand is that problems with external communication start with problems with our internal communication. You are programmed to talk that way. How can we talk better to others, if we don't know how to talk to ourselves?

We created this book and filled it with information on how to talk to yourself about your family, your career, your relationships, your spiritual guidance, and your money. There is power in your words, so choose the words you say to yourself carefully. What may start as a joke could become the way you describe yourself to others later.

We have been married for 10 years, and we are still on our honeymoon. Our married life is exactly like it was when we were dating, because we never stopped dating. Do you remember what going out was like when you dated? You were kind, you did special things for each other, you talked about your hopes and dreams. For some, you had intimacy and sex! You were happy and felt good about yourself because someone desired you. You had courage to try new things. We vowed to continue to respect, appreciate, love, cherish, and listen to one another, and 10 years later, we are still keeping that promise. Do you want blissful, honeymoon years in your life? Even if you are not in a relationship currently, you can prepare yourself for a life of BLISS.

What does it mean to live a life of BLISS? **We define BLISS as the freedom to love and to be loved in abundance, with complete forgiveness, and without judgment.** To love and to be loved are two different ideas. 'To love' is giving of yourself unconditionally. 'To be loved' is allowing yourself to receive love unconditionally. Many times, we succeed at one of these concepts but not the other. Abundance means you have more than enough. Love overflows from you to others and from others to you when you have an abundance of love in your life.

Nelson Mandela said, "Having resentment against someone is like drinking poison and thinking it will kill your enemy." When you do not forgive someone and hold on to resentment, it is like taking poison yourself and hoping that the other person dies. You kill your own hopes and dreams. You block your own success, not theirs. When you do not forgive, this emotion grows like a cancer, causing pain for both sides. Complete forgiveness allows you to forgive yourself and start all over again with the same enthusiasm, as in the beginning.

We all know that feeling judged is not a positive experience for most people. Self-judgment puts you at a continuous disadvantage because in your mind, you are not living up to a preset standard. To remove the feeling of judgment, you need to understand how the preset standard was created. When you remove judgment, you are free to be who you were created to be.

To be in a relationship with yourself, where love, forgiveness and non-judgment is the norm, is an amazing feeling we call BLISS. We want everyone to have BLISS in their life. How successful your relationships are starts with what you believe about yourself. We have thousands of relations in our lifetimes. We have personal relationships with our family members and friends. We have business relationships with our boss, coworkers, employees, and other business people. There are other types of relationships we have with teachers, pastors, and mentors. Imagine if every time you interacted with someone, you felt loved, appreciated, respected, valued, and/or part of a divine intervention. If each interaction resulted in something amazing happening in your life, then you would be excited to start each day to see what new things unfold. You live your purpose, and you want that feeling for everyone you meet. This is BLISS.

This book teaches you how to use the power of your words to develop BLISS in your life. What your BLISS looks like will depend on what you want. When you learn how to TALK STRAIGHT, you will find your BLISS. B.L.I.S.S. is not only a feeling, but it is also our five-step process for finding BLISS. How simple is that to remember?

The 'B' stands for BOLD. Be bold in your decision making. Once you decide that you deserve and want to be happy and live a blissful life, then you can take the next step. The decision is yours. If you change your mind, you can change your thinking and thus, change your life. By implementing the suggestions in this book, you make a bold decision to produce changes in your life, today.

The 'L' stands for Leverage. Leverage your circumstances. Look at your life. Use the lessons you already learned or lessons from others to keep you from repeating your negative patterns. Often, our actions today are the result of events that happened in the past. If you stop and ask yourself, "Why are you doing this?" or "Why do I feel so strongly about that?" then you can find the deeper lesson. But you must do the work of digging deeper to seek greater understanding. We hope the stories in this book will show you how to leverage your own circumstances to improve your life and achieve BLISS.

The 'I' stands for Inspired. Take inspired actions. Insanity is doing the same things over and over and expecting different results. If you want to have a different outcome, you must take a different inspired action. Your lessons will become your inspiration to do something differently in order to get different outcomes. This book will give you examples of inspired actions you can take.

The first 'S' stands for Self. Put yourself first. When you focus on yourself and take the time to find your BLISS, then you will be able to help others. Some people will try to make you think you are being selfish. We agree, but you should be selfish in this case. You need to be selfish to take the time you need to put your life on the right track. Give yourself permission to get what you need. Once your life is on the right track, then you can help others. But you must focus on your problems and decisions first. It is hard to help others when you don't know how to solve your own issues. The best way to lead is by example. Put yourself first. This book can help you do your work.

The last 'S' stands for Start now. If you know what you need to do, why put it off for later? Don't wait until the kids grow up or when you have enough money in the bank or you feel you have enough time. By reading this book, you are starting now. By investing in yourself, you are starting now. The sooner you start, the more BLISS you will enjoy in your lifetime.

TALK STRAIGHT DAMMIT utilizes these five steps to help you find your BLISS. No matter your gender, race, religious beliefs, or sexual preference, this five-step principle works. Whether you believe what we say or not, speaking negatively brings about negative results; speaking positively brings about positive results. TALK STRAIGHT is a tool to help you align with the universal laws which put into motion the power and abundance available to you. The Law of Attraction is real and works overtime, putting things in motion for you. This law is like gravity; it works whether you believe it or not, whether you are aware of it or not. A person becomes what they think, believe, and talk about, whether you recognize it or not. The Universe has an abundance of peace, joy, love, and BLISS. If your relationships could be filled with this kind of abundance, would you want it? Of course, you would! You must choose to believe in abundance to have it. There is no shortage in the universe. The difference between someone who has abundance and someone who does not is that the one with abundance chose to believe abundance exists.

Some of our beliefs about money make it hard for us to enjoy life. You might believe that you must struggle to get money. As a consequence of this belief, we attract the need to struggle through the Law of Attraction. The Law of Attraction occurs for both positive and negative beliefs. What happens to you in life boils down to the way you see life and what you believe about life. There was a time when my life spiraled downward. I was in financial hardship, going through a painful divorce, and unemployed. My thoughts attracted an abundance of negative outcomes. But I began to change my thoughts to focus on the things I wanted in my life. I began to say to myself, "I deserve better." A friend of mine sent me a video called, "The Secret." I watched that video over and over. "The Secret" taught me about the Law of Attraction by explaining how my negative thoughts attracted negative situations and how my positive thoughts attracted positive situations. I began to focus on what I wanted, not on what was going wrong or what I did not desire. Little by little, my circumstances began to change for the better. Good things started to happen faster and more often. By understanding the Law of Attraction and using it effectively in my life, I began to experience BLISS and live blissfully.

I ran into people who said, "I tried the Law of Attraction, but it did not work for me." Well, if they really understood the principles, then they would see that the Law of Attraction was working for them. They attracted negative situations and did not know how to stop. We often get so focused on problems happening in our life, we don't even know what makes us happy or how to be happy. We just want the pain and drama to stop. As a result of reading this book, you will produce a greater sense of purpose and direction which will attract the results you say you want. This book will help turn obstacles into opportunities, help you to increase your self-esteem, and improve your relationships. You say that you have a high self-esteem already? Well this book will help you improve your self-esteem even more. We recommend that you work on one area at a time so that you can see the impact of your work. By living by these principles, you can start to form your own Blissful life.

We are not licensed therapists. We don't have clinical degrees. But we can help you to leverage your circumstances, so you can see the possibilities. How successful you are at how you TALK STRAIGHT depends on how open and honest you are with yourself and how willing you are to try to think differently.

But don't just stop with this book. We encourage you to check out our website at www.MyBlisstopia.com where we created Blisstopia University, a place where you can go to find courses, tools, and tips to create BLISS in your life. You can also follow us at Facebook.com/myBLISStopia/. You will find live videos, free downloads, and many more tips and actions. If you feel you would like someone to help hold you accountable, we are available to provide life coaching. The more you tell yourself to TALK STRAIGHT, and the more people around you remind you to TALK STRAIGHT, the faster you will create BLISS in your life.

CHAPTER ONE

ARE YOU TALKING YOURSELF TO DEATH?

Stephen

Do our words really carry that much weight? There is a scripture that says, "Death and life are in the power of the tongue." (Proverbs 18:21 KJV). We realized over the course of our lives that good things happened when we spoke positively and believed them. The opposite was also true. We saw how our lives spiraled out of control when we believed negative thoughts. In this chapter, we will explain how negative thoughts, words, and actions can kill our hopes and dreams, and how positive thoughts, words, and actions can give us new life and a world of BLISS.

In the past, I found myself ruminating and catastrophizing. Ruminating relives an event through thoughts, words, and feelings about past hurts and disappointments. Catastrophizing predicts the worst possible outcome for a situation. Often both actions occur together. When combined, they accelerate your downward spiral, like pouring gasoline on a fire. The more gas, the hotter and faster the destruction.

Ruminating about negative events causes you to repeat those events and the pain they caused in your mind. You relive those negative emotions repeatedly each time you tell the story. Your mind does not know the difference between perceived thoughts and actual events. When rape victims tell their stories, they feel every emotion, as if it were happening all over again. Just saying the words can make the victims feel sick to their stomachs. They can feel their skin start to crawl from the thought of the rapist touching them. The tears start to flow. Add to this pain the anxiety from catastrophizing and your mind becomes stuck in negativity.

Catastrophizing draws the worst possible conclusion of a present or past situation based upon a negative belief and applies those conclusions to future events. For example, because planes have crashed, some people are afraid to fly, for fear that every plane that they get on in the future may crash also. The data actually shows that people are more likely to get killed in a car accident than they are to die in a plane crash. So why are they not afraid to drive a car? The story in their head is that driving is safer than flying because they are in control of the car but not the plane. Their belief about flying impacts their decisions today. Imagine all the wonderful adventures they miss out on because they can only go where their car can take them. This limiting belief or fear is how catastrophizing limits the BLISS they have.

Stephen

Wife No. 3

The fear of growing old and being alone without any family, other than my three girls in

Milwaukee, drove me to marry Wife No. 3. I refer to her as Wife No. 3 in order to protect her privacy.

As my second marriage ended, I was afraid that no one would be with me to take care of me. Wife No. 3 was a comforting soul who helped me get through the long divorce process of Wife No. 2. My fear drove me to marry her too soon, without knowing what I was getting myself into. My second marriage had barely ended before I jumped head first into this new relationship. Our romance was a very rocky road of constant breakups and make-ups that a person who saw clearly would have never taken. I should have followed my dad's advice that when a relationship is over, it is over. But I wanted to be with someone who I thought, at the time, appreciated me, even just a little. She told me all the things I wanted to hear; things that I did not get from Wife No. 2. So, I kept coming back for more, like a crack addict. That momentary high of feeling appreciated hid the ultimate destruction that was to come. I put up with many disrespectful actions that no person in their right mind would have even considered. My fear of being alone seemed so real in my head, at the time. I might have saved myself from much pain, if I had only taken the time to think things through.

I had many suspicions about her infidelities throughout our tumultuous relationship. Wife No. 3 often confessed that she had seen her ex-boyfriend, in what I thought was an attempt to make me jealous and try harder. Her visits with him seemed to occur more frequently on the weekends that I had my girls. In hindsight, I realized she was competing with my girls for my attention. But, whenever I could not find her, or she did not answer her home or cell phone, I ruminated that she was with her boyfriend, cheating on me. I felt the rage, anger, loneliness, sadness, and helplessness every time I thought about their relationship. What made the situation worse was my catastrophizing about what they were doing together. I imagined all the things that she and I did together and that he was taking my place in her life. As I spoke to friends about my concerns, the feelings came back all over again. The more I thought about it, the more miserable I felt.

On one particular night, after she did not answer either of her phones, I drove by her boyfriend's house around midnight. Yes, I knew where he lived. I saw that her car was parked outside. I was so infuriated. This was *my wife* at another man's house in the middle of the night. I went up to the door and rang the bell. I heard a male voice from behind the door say, "Who is it?" I answered, "Your girlfriend's husband." She appeared from behind the door. I don't remember much of the conversation, but I told her to go home.

The more times I could not find her, the more I imagined she was cheating. The real issue here was that although I was her husband, I had never moved in with her. Why? Because I did not trust her, and if she ever got mad and threw me out, I would not have a place for my girls to come and visit me. I know this sounds strange, but there were a lot of issues with this relationship. Cheating on me was just one concern.

Whenever we had an argument, she ran back to him. She also told me that I was lucky to have her in my life because I had young kids. The lie she told herself was that men with young kids were not as attractive on the dating scene. I always ignored statements like this, but in hindsight, maybe I should have paid more attention to her words. She was really telling me that the time I took to care for my kids was taking too much time away from her, without coming out and saying it directly.

This attitude became clear for me on the day her van was impounded. She had loaned her van to her ex-husband, without my knowledge. That's right her ex-husband! Yes, I know. I chose to ignore the signs that this marriage was doomed. Her ex-husband got a ticket and failed to pay it, so the city towed her van while it was still in his possession. As the owner, she was required to retrieve it from the impound lot. I took off early from my job to take her to pick up the van. Now, if you have ever had your car impounded, you know that it always takes more time than you planned to get your car. Trying to be helpful, I stayed with her. I remember this was a Wednesday, the day I picked up my girls for our mid-week visit. I never, ever skipped my visits with my girls. You could set your watch to the day and time I picked up my girls. And I was not about to let Wife No. 3's problem with her van make me late or miss picking up my girls.

As it got closer and closer to the time I needed to leave, I kept a watchful eye on the clock. I knew how long it would take me to get across town in rush-hour traffic. When she observed me watching the clock, she sarcastically commented, "I bet you won't be late picking up your girls." For some strange reason, she thought I should stay to help her out of the mess she created and miss picking up my girls. What I forgot to mention was that it was the last possible day to get the van back before the city put it up for sale. Why she waited until the last day, I don't know, and I didn't give a shit. I left her there waiting for her van and went to pick up my girls.

What she did not know was that her statement about how I wasn't going to be late to pick up my girls was the last straw. She crossed a line and there was no going back. My girls were the most important thing in my life. She put herself in direct competition with them for my attention. To borrow a line from the 1980's TV comedy show *In Living Color,* "Homey don't play that!" I needed someone in my life that helped me be a better father to my girls, not competed against them. Although it took a few more months to end the marriage, I was done. I wish she had loaned the ex-husband her car sooner; it would have saved me a couple of months from this 11-month disaster of a marriage.

Throughout this ordeal, I described these events over and over to my dear friend Lisa, and my sister Karen. Lisa and I have been the best of friends through all my relationships and all her relationships. I also told the story to anyone who would listen. I ruminated about the story of my failed marriage so many times, until one day, I was tired of hearing myself complain. I learned that talking about my situation was helpful, but talking about it so much that I was tired of hearing it did not help my situation. Recognizing when I start to ruminate more quickly and doing something about the problem, rather than repeating the story, allows me to return to BLISS. Sonji and I have BLISS today because we don't ruminate over our mistakes or catastrophize about our past relationships.

How many times do we punish ourselves, reliving the emotions of negative experiences? In some strange way, ruminating was my way of punishing myself for getting into that marriage. We are taught that if we do bad deeds, we should be punished. If we forgive ourselves, then we have no need to further punish ourselves.

What I did not know at the time was that the more I expected the worst from Wife No. 3, the more she made me right. The universe makes whatever you focus on become your reality. How you can change this outcome is by choosing to react differently to the situation. You can react negatively or positively. A positive reaction that I could have chosen would have been to leave the relationship completely. Leaving would have saved me months of heartache and heartbreak. Another positive reaction could have been to set clear rules and boundaries with consequences for breaking them. The more you repeat your choice, the more that outcome occurs. This repetition is how we attract the outcomes we want into our lives. When I finally chose a different reaction to Wife No. 3, I changed my outcome and my life.

When you ruminate and catastrophize, they begin to affect your body and your mental state. In some cases, sickness and depression set in, and in the worst cases, suicidal thoughts start to occur. Your health starts to deteriorate if you focus on these negative images too long. Your mind says, "Poor me," and your body agrees. When you say things like, "I can't get out of bed," or "I am just sick about it," your body will do everything in its power to prove you right. This negative self-talk is what we mean when we say, "Are you talking yourself to death?" When you get to the point of considering suicide, you have literally talked yourself to death.

Stephen

To live or not to live? That is my question

My supervisor called me to tell me to come to his office. I thought how strange the request was because I was a field-service technician that rarely came to the head office. He would not tell me what the meeting was about. The ride was 35 minutes, but it seemed like the drive took forever. I went over in my mind the recent events that warranted a visit to the office. I began to catastrophize. Did a customer complain? Was the company finally getting rid of the last African-American field technician? The other two were let go within the previous six months.

My fear came true. Not only was I laid off for the second time since coming to Milwaukee, I was told I was the worst mechanic they had. I was devastated by this statement. All I had in that moment was my reputation. I could get another job with a good reputation. I was not a terrible mechanic, but I knew someone else's wrong opinion could keep me from finding work. Their racism and jealousy were going to be a tough mountain to climb over.

I became depressed. I did not want to get out of bed. I didn't want to eat, so I lost a lot of weight. My circumstances were really bad, but they were worse in my head. I felt like I did not have any options. Without a college degree, all I could do was technical and manual work which broke my body down. I had previously had rotator cuff surgery on one shoulder and was scheduled to have the other shoulder repaired in a few weeks from work-related injuries. I did not know how long my body would hold up. I could not keep up this very demanding work; climbing ladders, crawling under, in, and out of boilers, or moving motors and compressors. With my physical abilities, I wondered how employable I would be. Without a job, I could lose my apartment. I would not have a place for my girls to come and see me.

At the time, my three little girls, whom I love dearly, were caught in the middle of another failed marriage I helped to create. How would this affect them? How would I be able to provide for them? When they came over for our weekend visit, I only got out of bed to feed them. Olivia, my oldest, who was age eight at the time, looked after her two younger sisters and periodically checked on me. No eight-year-old child should be placed in such a role. She doesn't remember helping so much but today, she still feels she must take care of her sisters. I take responsibility for my role in her feeling accountable for them today, yet I am so grateful for her willingness to help during that dark period of my life.

I ruminated about how terrible things were in my life; behind on child support, owing thousands of dollars to the Federal and State IRS. I could only catastrophize about more failure in my future. How could I find another high-paying job to ease my financial woes? This worry drove me to have real thoughts about suicide. Turn out the lights and call this party over. I believed I would not have to face my failures if I ended it all.

But how could I leave my girls to live without me? Somehow, I managed to keep getting up and putting one foot in front of the other for my sake and theirs. I love old sayings, and one that came to mind was, "I'll give out before I give up!" I could hear my grandmother cheering me on, "Stevie, I'm betting on you!" Through the pain, tears, and sleepless nights, and through being broke, busted, and disgusted, I persevered.

I attended therapy with my long-time therapist Dr. Martin-Thomas. I told her that once all the bills were paid and the troubles were passed, I would have time to enjoy life. She stated, "You don't have to wait until everything works out to enjoy life." Her statement was so profound to me. I came to the realization that all my problems did not have to be worked out before I started to enjoy life. I began to understand that I could have peace, joy, and happiness in the midst of my financial crisis. From that point on, I started telling myself a different story about me and my situation. I started shaping a new narrative, not only about my past but also about my present. I told myself that my situation was not as bad as I thought it was, and that life would get better. I started to be thankful, which took my mind off of the negative stories. What I did not know then, but what I know now, is that what you appreciate, appreciates. In other words, what you set your mind on grows in your consciousness. I thank Dr. Martin for planting that seed.

In this example, you can see how I nearly talked myself to death. I almost convinced myself that life was so bad, I was better off dead. In my mind, I believed my misfortune was so insurmountable that my actions began to make the adversity come true. Only after I began to see how my thoughts and words contributed to my worsening circumstances, could I begin to find solutions to the problem. Your situation may be different from mine, but I hope you see how ruminating and catastrophizing can talk you to death.

Having an attitude of gratitude was how I began to shift my negative thoughts into positive ones. Listing what you are thankful and grateful for is how you begin to TALK STRAIGHT. It is hard to ruminate and catastrophize when you are thankful and grateful. I was grateful that I was alive and, as Les Brown says, "Still in the game." I had my health, food to eat, a roof over my head, and my girls. You can write the things you are grateful down in a journal, on post-it notes, on your mirror, or in a text message to a supportive friend. Reflect on your blessings, multiple times throughout your day. Say what you are grateful for in the morning as you wake up, while you brush your teeth, on your drive to work, at lunch time, on your drive home, and before you go to bed at night. Filling your day with positive thoughts leaves very little room for ruminating and catastrophizing. Before you know it, you begin to produce BLISS on a continuous basis in your life.

Some unhealthy habits are easier to break than others. When circumstances don't go your way, it is easy to slip back into those old bad habits or project terrible outcomes into your future. My Aunt Lillie always told me, "Inch by inch, life is a cinch. Yard by yard, life is hard." You need to take life one step at a time, one sentence at a time; use baby steps. Celebrate the small wins, because they will, sooner or later, add up to a big win. Life is not about how many times you stumble and fall, but about how many times you get back up. As long as you get back up one more time than you fall, you can start over right where you are. Tell yourself that today will be better than yesterday, and tomorrow will be better than today. Doing this every day builds consistency, which creates a new healthy habit.

CHAPTER TWO

WHO TOLD YOU THAT?

Stephen

Our parents, family, friends, pastors, teachers, etc. have an enormous influence on us consciously and subconsciously. When we step back and look at the circumstances of our lives, often we want to blame others, ourselves, or both, if we are not getting the outcomes that we think we deserve. We need to know that we have the power to change the outcome of our lives by changing what we choose to believe. In this chapter, we will explore how what we were taught in the past affects our thoughts, words, and actions today.

Your thoughts direct your path. An example of this occurs in African American culture. African American men were told throughout history that there were certain things they could not do because of their race and gender. Many of us were taught to be suspicious of women, institutions, and other races. We heard phrases like, "Never trust anyone," "The system is set up so that you fail," and "Hide your money from your wife, or she will spend it all." So, when a boy grows up to be a man what does he do? He never trusts anyone, especially the police. He doesn't try for a promotion because he believes he will never get it anyway. He hides his money from his wife. He follows his programming, and it affects his adult life. But as an adult, he can choose to believe these ideas or not. The consequences of those beliefs belong to him, not his family or anyone else. If his wife leaves him because he hides money, he is responsible for his actions. When he can't find love because he never trusts anyone, he is responsible for this outcome. We must be 100% responsible for the outcomes of our decisions.

Changing your thoughts affects your words, changing your words affect your actions, and changing your actions affects your life. To change your thoughts or beliefs, you need to understand where your beliefs came from. You must figure out, "Who told you that?" Was it your drunk uncle who said, "Hide your money from your wife?" Maybe you should not listen to him. When you take in additional information about an old belief and you adjust your actions, you begin to change your life. One of the major influences in our lives is and will continue to be our families. Our identity, our thought patterns, and our way of being are greatly influenced by our families. We learn what is and what is not important from our families. Please keep in mind, we should not seek to blame anyone or even ourselves. But we must take an honest look at what is and what can happen to us if we make significant positive changes in our lives. We need to recognize that our families did and continue to do the best they can with the knowledge and consciousness they had at the time.

Sonji

We learn about ourselves, how to be in relationship with others, and how to handle life lessons from our families, friends, and others around us. Some beliefs we learned serve us well throughout our lives, yet others do not. Some information is a detriment to our success and well-being. You do not have to always agree with someone to love or respect them.

As children, we believe our parents. We trust them because they love us and have our best interest at heart. As long as they never hurt us, we usually do not question what they say to us. They teach us according to the life lessons they learned. As we grow up and become teenagers, we start to form new opinions from information we receive from people other than our parents. Learning to challenge the messages we have outgrown, in a healthy manner, can prove beneficial to your maturation and growth towards BLISS in your life.

One of the well-known facts about African Americans is that many do not go to get medical help until it is often too late. Most believe this choice is because they cannot afford the treatment. But a little-known fact from our history is that African Americans were the subjects of medical experiments. In the book, *Medical Apartheid* by Harriet A. Washington, there are many horrific stories about how slaves were used to test medical instruments without anesthesia, or how post-slavery African Americans were kidnapped off the streets, taken to the basements of hospitals, and released the next day, not knowing what happened to them, if they managed to survive the testing. You may have heard of the Tuskegee Experiment, where several African American males were given syphilis. Although a cure was discovered, the doctors decided not to treat the men, in order to study the full effects of the disease. These men were allowed to infect their families and die painful deaths, yet they were not recognized nor compensated for their contribution to medical history.

If an African American went to a hospital for an illness in the 1940's and 1950's, many were not treated properly, so that they could be used as body parts. *The Immortal life of Henrietta Lacks,* by Rebecca Skloot, tells the story of one African American woman whose cells were used to advance medical history. Henrietta's cells were the first cells to live outside of a human body for more than a few hours, which allowed researchers to test and create vaccinations and other medical testing procedures. However, her family was kept in the dark about her illness. When she went into the hospital to get treated for cervical cancer, she never returned. Now, if your grandparents knew of such examples of medical experimentation and decided that they would never go to a hospital or see a doctor because they didn't trust them, would you blame them for forming that opinion?

They instilled this same belief in your parents, who then instilled that belief in you as a child. Even if they had the money to go see a doctor, they might not. This old belief prevents many African Americans from seeking medical assistance and often results in premature deaths. Many grandparents and parents talked themselves to death because they chose to believe negatively about the medical profession today. How many stories do you know that were passed down from generation to generation that you still believe today? Even though you are not sure of their origins, they affect your behavior.

Sonji

No More Pacifiers

When my first child was born, my mother told me that I should not give him a pacifier. As a result of that conversation, I developed an opinion that pacifiers were bad. Children who used them had crooked teeth and often became dependent on them for a long time. I did not want to have to break my son of the habit later, so I did not use a pacifier. But my son cried, and I did not want him to cry. I stopped his crying by nursing him day and night. I saw how some parents got up and went into their babies' rooms to try to rock them back to sleep at night, but I was just too tired. I decided to put him in my bed and nurse him while I slept. This solution seemed like a win-win situation. I got sleep, and he could eat when he wanted and be quiet. This remedy was great, until his teeth started to decay.

What I didn't realize was that leaving milk on his teeth all night rotted my child's teeth, and that I should have brushed his baby teeth. No one showed me how to brush his teeth. A simple device could have helped. I didn't do a good job of brushing my own teeth. I hated going to the dentist because it took so long to clean my teeth, and he always found cavities. When I finally took my son to the dentist as he got older, the dentist said that all his front teeth were rotten. It is frightening for some adults to get just one tooth pulled. Imagine how it felt for my little boy to get all his upper and lower front teeth pulled! They only numbed the area surrounding his teeth and did not use anesthesia. He had to watch the lights, which were so bright, and hear the sounds of the drill while the hygienists held him down. To make matters worse, he had to go more than once to get all the work done. I felt I failed him. I could not be there while they hurt my baby. His father had to take him because I was too distraught. His pain was my fault.

As a result of this traumatic experience, he became terrified of bright lights and doctor's offices. Could you blame him? We could not even take a family photo because the photographer's lights reminded him of the dentist office. He immediately remembered the pain and started crying. I just gave up on family photos for a while.

For a long time, my son's smile was like a little vampire's. He had the little fangs remaining but no other front teeth. "Mom, when are my teeth going to grow back?" he constantly asked. It took nearly eight years for them to appear. I never knew that one simple decision to not use a pacifier would have such a drastic effect on my child's life. I blamed myself for years. Today, I understand that my mother was just giving the best advice she could with the information she had. I also came to realize that my decision was based on the information I had at the time also. I now take 100% responsibility for my decision and tell my story so that others can make a different decision.

I recently had a conversation about the pacifier with my mother. What she remembers about the event was different. She thought that she told me that I should not give my child a pacifier that had fallen on the floor and was dirty. If that was her intent, she did not state it clearly. Nevertheless, it was the story in my head that affected my behavior.

I learned from this situation that I needed to question the advice people gave me. I learned the principle of 'Trust but Verify' from my husband. The book *The Fifth Agreement*, by Don Miguel Ruiz, teaches us to listen but question. We should listen to the advice people give, but ask questions to determine if this same information is valid for our circumstances. I trust that my mother gave me the best advice she knew at the time, but it was my responsibility to verify the purpose of the pacifier. Your family will give you lots of advice. You must decide which information is worth keeping, and what advice you should ignore. I know that my family loves me, and they know I love them. I don't have to agree with a person to love them. Everyone walks in the light of the understanding they have.

People are right where they need to be based upon the journey they traveled. You are on a journey today, while reading this book, to help change the outcome of your life. People around you would need to have traveled the same journey that you did to have the enlightenment that you have today. So, love them right where they are, and continue your journey.

You may need to spend less time with some people who are negative or do not support your journey, until you become strong enough to resist their negative influence. Remember, the more you hear something, the more influence it has. Spending less time with negative influencers is a step in the right direction. When you can recognize the impact that negativity has on you and you learn how ignore it, then you are strong enough to spend more time in such situations. Set your standard for who you will spend your time with on your journey, and leave the rest right where they are. They are on their own paths. They might try to convince you to leave your journey and stay the way you are. Don't allow them to deter you from your journey towards BLISS.

Many people believe that BLISS is connected to having an abundance of money, yet money is seldom talked about. Some people find it difficult to talk about money. We learn about money mostly from watching and listening to our parents. By watching them, we learn what to do and what not to do with money. You may have seen your parents fight over money. This left a negative impression, so you refused to talk about money as an adult to avoid fighting. Some learn about money though a course or watching others. At work, we are told to never talk about how much money we make. If we compared paychecks, we might find that someone who does less work makes more money than we do. No matter how you learned about money, you probably have developed strong beliefs without really talking in-depth about the subject.

Most people who win the lottery or come into significant amounts of money end up poorer than when they started because of their monetary beliefs. If you were taught to invest the money, you will do that. If you were taught that you should help the poor, you will do that. If you were taught that people with money are self-centered, corrupt, and dishonest, you will find ways to get rid of the money so that people won't think that about you. Most people don't manage their money, and before they know it, they spend more or give more than the amount they received. How many of us are taught that, "Money doesn't grow on trees," or "You must work hard and save all your money," or that your father was "not made of money?" These concepts are often ingrained in us. When we grow up, even if our financial situation is different from our parents, we continue to use the same principles we were taught.

Sonji

Money Doesn't Grow on Trees

One day my coworker and I decided to go to lunch. I had just finished attending a 'Motivating the Masses' conference in San Diego. One of the topics at the conference was about money blocks. I learned that what I believed about money came from watching my parents. I asked my coworker what her parents taught her about finances. She started by saying, her parents were really good with money and saved a lot. She did not lack for anything when she was growing up. Her father sometimes said, "Money doesn't grow on trees."

I then asked her how her saving was going. Our company was going through its second downsizing. My coworker decided to cut back on her expenses for a while so that she could save every extra dollar. She even decided to sell her home and rent an apartment. In case she was selected for downsizing, she lowered her monthly expenses and met her goal for saving.

I then asked her, "How do you think your parent's beliefs about money affect you today?" She realized that she was doing exactly what her father did. She believed that money did not grow on trees and that there could be a scarcity of money in her near future. So, she saved, even to the point of sacrificing some of the activities she enjoyed, just in case. The reality is that you never know when a company is going to let you go. So rather than enjoying life and having BLISS, the beliefs of her father taught her to be afraid. This fear created stress in her life and robbed her of activities she enjoyed.

In the end, my coworker was not affected by the downsizing, but our conversation caused her to think differently. It is okay to "save for a rainy day," but don't let your fear about money affect your BLISS today. Although I faced the same situation as my coworker, I chose to continue living my life as it was before the announcement. I chose to not worry about the money. The story in my head was that money is abundant, and that if I lost that job, I would find another one. I have faced two downsizings by previous companies. I worried about money then, but not this time. I leveraged my past, so I knew that I would survive just fine.

Stephen

The Bible has a lot to say about money. For example, "It is easier for a camel to go through the eye of a needle than for a rich man to enter the Kingdom of God." (Mark 10:25 KJV) This Bible quote set up a narrative in my head about rich people. I really did not want to be rich because it made it infinitely harder for me to go to heaven. But how much was too much money?

Many of us learned that the root of all evil is money. The Bible actually says that the root of all evil is the LOVE of money. Either way, most of us just decide that money is evil. So, we bring this evil money into the storehouse or church and hopefully benefit others,

45

while serving the Lord with the money that is considered evil. If you are someone who truly believed that money is evil, this affected how you talked to yourself about money. As many of us know, monks, nuns, and priests take a vow of poverty and give up their worldly possessions. We view these people as the best examples of righteous or pious living. We believe that if we give our money away, then we to can be closer to God. Many of us subconsciously give our money away through wasteful spending, terrible investments, or not earning to our potential. If every time you get money and it runs through your hands like water, you should stop and think about how your beliefs affect the way you handle money.

The story in my head started to change. Rather than think money is evil, I started to ask, "How much more good work could I do if I had all the money the church needed?" I wanted to be the person that earned a lot of money so that I could help lots of people. To achieve this goal, I needed to stop thinking of money as evil and to TALK STRAIGHT about money. What worked for me may not work for you. If the way you think about money causes you problems, the only way to change your programming is to get additional information. Take a course, get a financial advisor, or read a book. There is so much information on handling and creating wealth.

For some, just like with money, often our religious beliefs are formed by our parents. Some of us never had a choice when were younger because our parents dictated which religion was followed in their house. When we grew up, we never changed our religion. Whether you believe in religion or you don't, at some point in your life, you made a decision about this topic, even if it was to keep your parents' religious beliefs. Your religious beliefs were shaped by whether you accepted or rejected religion. For example, you will not support financially a cause that is contrary to your religious beliefs. If you are not religious, you may choose not to support religious organizations. In both cases your religious beliefs affect your actions. It does not matter what you call your spiritual source: The Creator, The Universe, The Supreme Being, Allah, Jehovah, or Jesus. What does matter is how you perceive yourself in relationship to your spiritual source.

Stephen

The Temple

As a child, I was taught that we need to be saved to keep from going to hell. You must be perfect to go heaven. Since I was not perfect, I had to continuously ask for forgiveness and guidance so that I could be redeemed from my sins and still go to heaven. I was taught to be afraid of God. I was also told that he loved me and would forgive me if I asked. Because of religion, my mother taught me to be very judgmental about myself and others. I could only think that I was a poor, wretched sinner and that I needed to beg God's forgiveness. The battle in my head that I lived with for years was that because I was a sinner, I was never good enough for God.

As far back as I can remember, my mother took me from one church to another. I recall going to Baptist, Church of God, Methodist, Church of God and Christ, Pentecostal, Apostolic, and Non-Denominational churches, as well as others I don't even remember. Each denomination thought that their way was the only right way. We even visited Jim Jones' church in California.

Thank God she found something wrong with that one too!

Bible held an important place in my mother's house. It was the guide for every waking moment of action and thought. I was fascinated with its stories. My mother even tried to create her own version of the Bible and set of religious rules, then forced my sister and I to live by them. There was always a threat of punishment for transgressions against God's law. The ultimate punishment was eternal torture in the flames of hell. Hell was vividly described in the Bible as, 'the weeping and gnashing of teeth,' a place where you were tortured forever.

My mother made it sound like I had a choice as to which religion I could live by, but I really did not have any choice. She basically said, choose my religion or suffer eternal punishment in hell's fires. We believed all other religions were considered wrong and evil. Writing this chapter was hard for me because it reminded me of how I bought into this belief so thoroughly and completely. It pains me to see now how I use to think that there was only one path to God, and that I would never be worthy of his rewards. Changing my belief about God, church, and religion took me through the five stages of grief; denial, anger, bargaining, depression, and acceptance. It took a lot of time and work to redevelop my spiritual foundation of love, trust, and acceptance of myself. When I got older, I studied the Bible and became an ordained minister. As I continued to study and grow, I understood the Creator is much bigger and more powerful than any one religion.

I have been very fortunate to travel to several places around the world. One of my dreams was to visit India, which I finally had the opportunity to do. India had a particularly profound effect on me. My wife and I visited the Lotus Temple in New Delhi, and everyone was so respectful, kind, and courteous. There were people from all the major faiths of the world; Hindus, Muslims, Christians, Buddhists, Sikhs, Baha'i and Judaism followers were all represented, as well as other religious beliefs I was not familiar with. What was fascinating to me was that no one tried to recruit anyone to their religious preference. I could feel the oneness of all people. Visiting the Lotus Temple validated my belief that God loves all his people.

We are not trying to change your belief in religion. We want you to use your religious beliefs to empower you by focusing on the positive lessons of religion. Love is what really matters. I personally love the Creator and all creation. Loving oneself is paramount to your ability to love others. Most people see the world as they see themselves. If you see yourself as always lacking, you will see the same in others. Loving kindness is something we need to give ourselves. This love is how you TALK STRAIGHT about religion to yourself.

With all these religious rules in my head, how did I find BLISS? I made a conscious effort to focus on the positive principles of religion, which did not take place overnight, but over several years. I began to tell myself a new narrative about my spiritual source. Slowly, I came to understand that I was in a loving relationship with the Creator and that this relationship was a supportive and nurturing one. I TALK STRAIGHT to myself by saying I am accepted just as I am. I released negative judgment against myself and others, which was not easy, and the journey of forgiveness really began to open me up to BLISS.

The Bible says, "Judge not least ye be judged." (Matt 7:1 KJV) I always thought that this statement meant for me to not judge others. But the verse's true meaning is about how we judge ourselves. When I pass judgment on someone else, it is because I judge myself so harshly. When I finally stop judging myself, then and only then, can I stop judging everyone else. All of us are looking for that safe space where we are not judged by others. When someone judges me outwardly, I try not to take things personally. 'Do not take things personally' is the second agreement in the book by Don Miguel Ruiz called, *The Four Agreements*. I know that when someone judges me, they are really judging themselves, so I choose to have compassion for them instead of resentment. Don't focus on the words they say to you. Reject the negativity and change the wording in your head. By not taking it personally, their negative energy does not get into you.

As I began to forgive those around me, the past, and even my own decisions, the love that had existed inside me all the time began to spring forth in little ways. I found more enjoyment around me. I began to develop a more peaceful and loving way of being. Funny things started happening as I continued to grow in BLISS. People randomly started having conversations with me out of the blue in public. I believe that as my confidence grew, people saw me as being approachable. My wife jokingly said, "Turn off your face because I am tired of these strangers talking to us." Eventually the BLISS rubbed off on her, and more and more people struck up conversations with her as well. People can see when you genuinely love the Creator, yourself, and others.

The Fifth Agreement, by Don Miguel Ruiz, says to be skeptical but learn to listen. The next time your family, friends, pastors, or coworkers try to fill your head with their negative beliefs, ask yourself the following questions:

1) Who told you that?

2) What if that was not a true statement?

3) What would happen if I chose a different path?

Recognizing that our programming affects our decisions is the first step to TALK STRAIGHT to ourselves. The Bible says in Philippians 4:8, "In conclusion, my friends, fill your minds with those things that are good and that deserve praise, things that are true, noble, right, pure, lovely, and honorable." The Bible tells us how to TALK STRAIGHT by filling our minds with those elements listed in Philippians.

CHAPTER THREE

HOW TO TALK
STRAIGHT

Stephen

Now that we understand how others helped form what we think about ourselves and believe, how can you begin to TALK STRAIGHT to yourself? The first thing is to take a deep breath and realize you are not alone. You are not here by accident. You are exactly where you should be, doing exactly what you need to do. You are here because of your thoughts, words, and actions. When you put your life together in the order you did, the result is exactly where you are today. You did the best you could do with the information and resources you had. To get from where you are today to where you want to be in the future, you must take 100% responsibility. Know that you got yourself to where you are, and you can get yourself where you want to be.

People used to think if you talked to yourself, you were going crazy. But we actually talk to ourselves all the time. The voice you hear when you are alone or about to make a decision is your own. What does that conversation look like? Do you lift yourself up or put yourself down? Do you predict a positive outcome or a negative one? There is power in the words you speak and the words that you say in your head. We all know how a simple or off-handed comment can either make or destroy your day in a moment. We easily accept the power of someone else's words, but we ignore the power in our own words and thoughts. I challenge you to listen and observe your thoughts and words, as well as the thoughts and words of others. You will probably find that most thoughts, whether yours or someone else's, are overwhelmingly negative and limiting. If you pay attention to the negative thoughts coming at you from inside and outside, for 365 days a year, multiplied by the number of years you have lived, you can understand how hearing negative remarks that long can affect your thinking. You must take charge of your thoughts and words and reject the thoughts and words of others that are negative. To move from where you are now to where you want to be will take some time.

Consider the story about how to boil a frog. If you heat up the water first and drop the frog in, it will jump out immediately. If you place the frog in the cool water first and then turn up the temperature slowly, the frog will adjust and not notice that it is being cooked. Our negative thinking is like turning the temperature up slowly. We hardly notice when someone says something negative any longer because we have agreed with the negativity in our own minds for so long. First, they say, "You are stupid." You might joke or laugh the comment off several times, but gradually, eventually you begin to believe it. Then you say to yourself how stupid I am for doing something wrong or a task incorrectly. You start repeating these criticisms over time; when you forget the groceries in the car, when you drop the spoon, you say, "Stupid me." And finally, the negative thoughts are no longer a joke but your reality.

Sonji

The same happens with positive comments. As a little girl, if your father said how beautiful you were every day, you believed him. You believed him so much that to this day, you won't let anyone say that you are ugly. You say, "I am beautiful," each time you look in the mirror. When anyone tries to convince you that you are anything less than beautiful, you say, "Girl, bye!" Imagine how saying positive things to yourself every day could eventually deprogram the negative thoughts in your mind. You may have to say positive affirmations consistently over the course of years before you can erase negative thoughts. Positive affirmations are worth the time investment. After all, finding your BLISS is worth it.

To TALK STRAIGHT, half the battle is recognizing when negative comments are said about you, by yourself and others, then rejecting them. If you recognize the negativity, you can replace the words in that moment with positive words. Recognizing the negative and replacing with the positive takes a lot of practice.

Sonji

Too Skinny

I used to be really skinny when I was younger. I was 95 pounds for most of my teenage years. I was so skinny that kids made fun of me. My parents used to be members of a Citizen Band-Radio Club, which was a way to talk to people across the country. Instead of giving your name each member created a "handle" or nickname. My father and my mom were Spider Man and Spider Lady. I chose the handle "Sticks" because I knew I was so skinny. I even drew a walking stick as my body on my pretend business cards.

As I got older, I hated being skinny. The worst point was when I was rejected by the military because I did not weigh enough. I tried everything I could to gain the 10 pounds I needed to meet the minimum weight requirements. I tried eating unhealthily; I worked at Burger King and ate fast food every chance I could. I even tried drinking protein shakes that helped people gain weight. Nothing worked.

That inability to gain weight all changed after I had my children. It took me many years, but I succeeded at gaining weight. My doctor actually, told me that I needed to lose weight. Suddenly, I wished I was thinner. When I looked in the mirror at exercise class, I saw myself looking like my mother. I love my mother and she is a beautiful woman, but the more weight I gained, the more I looked like her. I wanted to be my own person.

You see, my thoughts dictated how I felt about my body, and my feelings guided my actions to gain weight. I finally realized that being thin or overweight was not the issue. Being happy with who I am was the issue. And I believed that I was not enough. I wanted more; more weight, more acceptance for who I was, more money. Our weight is just an external symptom of the internal issue we have with ourselves. Before we can lose or gain weight, we need to address our internal conversation. Otherwise we will just find something else that we are not satisfied with.

What I say to myself now is that I am healthy and beautiful, inside and out. My gratitude and appreciation for what is allows me to focus on enjoying life and making healthy choices. Now, I enjoy the outdoors, keep up with my family on outings, and savoring every morsel I put in my mouth.

Your environment can direct how you speak to yourself. If you hang around negative people, they will start to affect your outlook on life. You need positive and supportive people in your life to help you become positive. We usually imitate life around us. As we grew up, we watched our role models, maybe your parents or other relatives, movie stars or athletes. You modeled or rejected certain actions and behavior based upon watching them. Ask yourself what your parents taught you, and you will begin to see the programming in your life. Did you decide you were never going to spank your children because of the spanking you received from your parents? Ask yourself what your friends do that you imitate? Do you and your friends like to go out and get drunk every Friday night? This mirroring is how programming works.

Most religions teach about being 'unequally yoked,' the idea that you shouldn't marry someone from another religion because they don't share your beliefs. The concept of being equally yoked is bigger than just being married, but rather about who in your life influences you. You are yoked (attached) to your teachers, your bosses, your grocery market clerk, your mechanic, your doctor, your employees, your co-workers, your friends, and so on. The people around you help form your opinion of the world and how you view yourself. If you were unjustly sent to prison for a period of time, eventually, you would begin to think and act like those who you were locked up with, so that you could survive in that environment. Momma use to say, "Be careful who your friends are." If you hang around smart people you will act like smart people. Why do you think we enroll in universities? We want to be doctors, therapists, or teachers, so we study the things they know and volunteer or intern where they work, so we can understand how to be like them. If I want to change my current environment to a different one, then I need to find a more desirable environment that is in alignment with the future I want.

What we fail to realize is how toxic some environments can be. The wrong surroundings can take a positive person and change them into a negative one over time, just like the frog in the pot of water. Sometimes it is better and healthier for you to just stay away from toxic environments if you can. People who join a church usually stop going to the night club to avoid the environment. They spend more time at church, fellowshipping with other members. Recovering alcoholics stop going to the bars or visiting friends who drink a lot, so they are not tempted. They spend more time in AA meetings or with other recovering alcoholics.

If you can't eliminate the toxic people from your life, then limit your time around them. Stephen often tells me, "We can't fix our friends and family unless they are willing to receive our coaching and do the work." What we can do is fix ourselves, and hopefully when they see our results, they may decide to do their work as well.

Stephen

The 80/20 rule

Until recently in my life, I did not realize how the words others said to me affected how I lived my life. A few of my employees told me that I did not know how to "talk to people" at work. I supervised 19 people, but three of them were not happy. I began to believe this negative message over time because I did not reject it in my mind. I could not sleep because this statement was contrary to what I knew myself to be. I have been a talker most of my life. Some say I have the gift of gab, and I utilized my gifts as a minister in the church, as a comedian, and as a technical instructor. In all three activities, I was well received and considered to be an excellent orator.

When I arrived at this company, most of the workers were not used to being told what to do. They could do what they wanted and were not held accountable for the results. I began to implement processes to hold the employees accountable. These changes were not received well, initially. At times, I was threatened by some of my direct reports. They spoke profanity and disrespected me in front of other employees. Each time I tried to give instructions or correct their mistakes, they ran to my boss and misrepresented what I said, in hopes of getting me fired.

Even though many of the unhappy employees left the company, the constant complaints of how I talked to them began to take its toll in the way I perceived myself and performed my job. I stopped caring about what happened at the company because it seemed that my manager did not support my efforts. The employees who were supportive of me noticed that I shrank in my role as a leader and did less teaching and coaching. I stopped sharing my gifts and talents. I no longer liked my job and kept looking for other employment opportunities where I could be valued.

Fortunately, my wife and friends knew and appreciated my gifts and talents. They encouraged me and put positive thoughts about my life back into my head, when I could not see my value. My wife told me every morning that I was a great boss, husband, father, and friend. She and my friends reminded me how I made a difference in the lives of the residents in the housing developments for which we were responsible, providing them a safe and functional environment to live. They showed me how I was spending 80% of my time focusing on 20% of my problems. So, I started to focus on the 80% of my employees that did want to listen to what I had to say.

The conversation in my head changed from, "These people don't appreciate me, and I need to find a new job," to "I am making a difference in the lives of those around me, and I do know how to talk to people." I continued to work at the same company, and my work environment changed over time, as I learned to focus on what I did right, not what I did wrong. I returned to my old self, and the employees that were supportive of me noticed the difference. The 80% started enjoying our workplace even more. Most of the 20% that caused previous problems either left or climbed on board the positive train.

I realize that there will always be someone in my life who will not accept the positive person I continue to become. I remember hearing a statement from Jack Canfield that other people's negative opinion of me is none of my business. What I think about myself is what really matters.

People often ask us how to stay positive in a negative environment. We tell them to practice…, practice…, practice. Practice being positive and seeking those who encourage you. You have trained yourself so long at being negative that you need to learn a new skill, which eventually becomes an unconscious action. It does not matter how many times you fail, as long as you keep trying to succeed. If you find yourself saying negative things about yourself and others, forgive yourself and start again. Thomas Edison failed 10,000 times while inventing the light bulb. Start by creating an affirmation using "I am …" statements. One of the affirmations by Charles Haanel that we say is, *"I am whole, perfect, strong, powerful, loving, harmonious, and happy."* We have this affirmation posted in our bedroom on our vision board, and I have a picture of it in my phone. We say it several times throughout the day, and I have committed it to memory. When I hear myself saying negative statements, I turn them into positive ones.

Create your own list of positive affirmation statements. Post them on your mirror, in your car, at your desk, on your phone, etc. Tell your friends who are encouraging to remind you when they hear you speak negatively. Over time, you will begin to hear yourself TALK STRAIGHT. You may need to adjust your statements from generic platitudes to new, more specific possibilities.

TALK STRAIGHT EXAMPLES	
Negative	Positive
I am never on time	I am always on time
I am never going to get a promotion	I am valued, respected, and appreciated
I can't lose weight	I eat healthy and lose weight
I don't have enough money	I have enough money to do everything I need to do

TALK STRAIGHT EXAMPLES	
Negative	Positive
I don't have enough time	I have plenty of time, and I use it wisely
A woman's work is never done	I accomplish everything I need to
Nobody treats me right	I have rewarding and fulfilling relationships
Nobody loves me	I love me and so do others

It may be hard for you to believe these statements, at first. They may seem outrageous and unrealistic. Don't be discouraged when you don't see immediate results. The more you say these positive messages and see circumstances start to change, the more you will begin to believe them. Others will also begin to see a difference in you. Some will like the change, others will not. Some will try to convince you that you cannot change your circumstances, but that is the thinking that got you to where you are right now.

Stick with the program of positive affirmations. This exercise is not a one-and-done process. It is a life-style change.

How do you embrace change? Do you focus on the negative aspects? Or do you try to find the positive? Even in unexpected change, you can find beauty and lessons. Changes in life help you become either resilient and resourceful, or resentful and bitter. The choice is yours. The more you TALK STRAIGHT to yourself, the more beauty you will see in your past, present, and future.

Stephen

Life Beyond My Control.

It was June 1969, in Suffolk, Va. The school year was over. It was like any other summer vacation day, except life as I knew it was about to change. I was only eight years old, when my mother called my sister Sheilah, who was a year and a day older than I, and me into the living room to sit down on the couch. All I remember being told by my mother was that she was sick, and my sister and I were going to live with our father in California. Hearing the words, "going to live with your father," was both exciting and scary at the same time.

My mother had suffered a nervous breakdown, due to a mental condition called schizoaffective disorder, which is both bipolar and schizophrenia. At the time, all I knew was that she spent a lot of time in bed. My dad was 32 years old and recently re-married, when out of the blue, he got the call from my mother saying she could no longer care for his kids and to come and get them. Luckily for me, he chose to take responsibility for us. He had to tell his new wife that his two small children were coming to live with them. I am not sure how that conversation went, but I do know he showed up with two tickets for us that same day.

Moving to a new place became the norm for my sister and me. We had just moved from Murfreesboro, NC to Virginia only six months earlier, which was 35 miles down the road from my grandma, granddaddy, and most of my aunts, uncles, and cousins. We had moved to North Carolina from Springfield, MA only 18 months earlier. Moving was a regular occurrence, but now, my sister and I had to move to California! That was almost 3,000 miles away from everyone I knew and loved.

I don't ever remember seeing my father until the day he came to take us to California. There he stood, a tall, light brown man with black curly hair. Although he was 5'5" tall, which is short to most people, to an eight-year-old, he looked tall. I was excited that I was going to live with dad! Every little boy wants to know his dad, and I was no different. I was also excited about going on my very first airplane ride. You see, I wanted to be a pilot; I liked planes and I thought flying one was cool. Once the initial shock and terror of moving to California all subsided, I began to embrace the future with excitement and enthusiasm.

As I leaned into this new situation, I started to learn and grow. My dad signed me up for Cub Scouts. I entered my first, and last, soap-box derby. I got a chance to participate in a pitch, hit, and throw contest that was sponsored by Phillips 66. My dad and I practiced in the evenings after he came home from work. Most kids that grow up without their father dream of throwing the ball around together. At last, I was living my new reality.

I got my first job, working with my dad, cleaning office buildings on the Air Force Base. We swept and dusted, emptied ash trays, and waxed floors. I even learned how to use a floor-buffing machine, though I remember being dragged across the floor several times by this machine that was bigger than I was. My dad taught me how to balance the machine to control the direction. He taught me how to wash and wax a car, which I applied to my bicycle. He even taught me to cook, since he was a sergeant in the Air Force, and oversaw the officer's mess hall. I was even given the responsibility of cutting the grass with a gas-powered lawn mower. That year, at the age of eight, I learned so many things with my dad. Some may say that he should have been arrested for violating child labor laws, but for me, the time my dad spent teaching me was priceless. This was something I never knew before. I could have complained about all the work he made me do; I could have rebelled and said, "Why do I have to do all these chores? Mom never made me do it." But I embraced the change and leveraged my situation, even at this early age. Little did I know, at the time, how useful this way of thinking would be for the rest of my life.

Writing this story today, I now see my father in a different light. For most of my life, I pointed out that my dad was only present in my childhood for two of the 18 years. Although this statement is a true, what I realize now is that he was there when I needed him. He provided me a place to live when my mom was sick. At the time, I did not fully understand the circumstances of my parent's break-up, but I am thankful that he chose to come and get me when I needed him.

As you look back over your life with a grateful heart, you learn to be thankful for how you got to be where you are today. Because you are reading this today, it means you are still alive. In the words of the rapper Ice Cube, that means, "Today was a good day." You are able to TALK STRAIGHT by taking what most might think was a bad situation and leveraging it in a positive light. You might struggle to be positive the first time you recall the situation, but over time and like for me, as months and years pass, you will learn how to tell a different story that helped to propel your life in the direction of your dreams, rather than away from them. This process does not mean that once you learn to TALK

STRAIGHT, bad things won't happen. But very few situations in life are fatal. As they say in church, "Trouble don't last always." Whatever you are dealing with, you can leverage the narrative, and find a way to be thankful and grateful for the experience, knowing it can help to make you better in the long run.

Sonji

When Stephen and I started this journey, we called the amazing positive events that happened to us the 'Millet Magic.' People offered us free stuff, such as concert tickets for artists like Diana Ross, Roberta Flack, Jill Scott, and various comedians. When I heard that Diana Ross would be in town, I thought to myself how I would like to see her. I never told anyone my desire, yet three days later a friend called and said she could not attend, but if wanted her tickets, I could have them for free! Another time, we were paid $2600 in cash for being bumped off a full flight. We recognized the small things as well, like having the best parking spots open as we pulled up; strangers giving us complements; and having perfect weather for outside events we hosted. The point is that when we expect and speak positive things into our lives, we continue to manifest the benefits. We appreciate and celebrate the little victories and show gratitude for everything.

Both affirmations and gratitude work together to bring about your desired results. What you appreciate increases and what you celebrate gets repeated. Think of gratitude as the X-factor. Gratitude multiplies and accelerates your results. We encourage you to test this process. The worst that can happen is that nothing changes for you, but the best that can happen is that your life will improve dramatically. You will begin to see yourself and your life through new and exciting ways. As you TALK STRAIGHT DAMMIT and change the conversation in your head, your life will change.

CHAPTER FOUR

LET'S TALK STRAIGHT ABOUT SEX AND RELATIONSHIPS

Sonji

Let's take what we learned in the previous chapters and apply those lessons to one of the most difficult topics to talk about, SEX. In this chapter we will talk about the thoughts in our head that we have about sex and relationships and learn how those thoughts can affect our actions and sexual conversations. The stories in our head about sex can either prevent us from enjoying sex or increase our pleasure of sex. When left to our own devices, we create stories about sex that may be inaccurate. Life would be so much easier if we talked about sex in a healthy way.

We all have our own reasons why we do not talk about sex. Talking about it may be taboo in some cultures. It may dredge up a bad memory or remind us of a former great relationship. For those who are religious, thinking sexual thoughts might bring about the feeling of sinfulness. The bottom line is, how do you feel about your sexuality? If you are happy with your sex life, then this chapter will help to confirm what you believe and enhance it even more. If you are unhappy with your sex life, then this chapter may help you improve your outcome.

What we think about sex is often formed early in our lives. The experiences we had and the information we received formed our opinions about sex. Maybe we saw people having sex in a movie. As teenagers, we heard our friends talking about sexual conquests or their first experiences. If you were lucky, you got "The Talk" when you turned a certain age. In school, health class taught us about our bodies. In church, we learned bad girls had sex, good girls did not. There was the story of Sodom and Gomorrah in the Bible. I was taught these places were destroyed for having sex and doing immoral things. All I took away from the story was that God destroyed those cities because of sex.

For many of us, men and women, our first encounters with sex were mentally and/or physically traumatizing. One out of four of women have experienced some form of sexual assault, of which, I am sad to say, I am one. Even when you haven't encountered a traumatic experience, sex is still difficult to talk about. Add to the traumatic experience, incorrect programming, and you might not ever let the word 'sex' come out of your mouth.

Sonji

The Sitter

When I was in elementary school, I was molested by a sitter. Before I even knew what sex was, I was having it. One day at school in health class, I learned about how babies were made. The realization made me sick to my stomach; not because it was gross, but because I worried if I was pregnant. The boy sticks his private in the girl and she becomes pregnant. That was the information I learned. I did not know that I needed my female cycle first to get pregnant, but I worried every day.

Sex to me, at that time, was a game I played in my bedroom with the sitter. I just laid there like a dead fish while the sitter did some weird things to my body. Occasional he made me do something to him. After the game, I was rewarded with things I wanted, like cookies. It was a game I never told anyone about, or he would get in trouble and be mad with me. Although I did not like the game, it made me feel special because the sitter was nice to me and gave me special treatments. Every child wants to be thought of as the favorite by someone.

That day in school when they talked about sex in health class, I asked my friends, "Do you really believe that stuff the teacher said?" "Yes, my cousin was talking to her friend, and they said the same thing." "I heard grown-ups talking and they said only bad girls have sex," another friend added. My friends did not know about my game with the sitter. I started to feel so ashamed. I did not want to be a bad girl. I figured if I stopped and I wasn't pregnant already, then I would not become pregnant.

I started to hate playing the game and cried when he made me. He bribed me more to stop me from crying. I don't remember how many times we played the game in all, but after that health class, I did not want to play anymore.

One day my period came, and mom took me to the doctor for my first female exam. The doctor asked me in the exam room if I ever had sex. He said to tell him the truth because he would find out. So, I did. Little did I know, he told my mom that I had something I should tell her. On the way home, she kept trying to get me to talk about whatever the doctor thought she should know, so I told her. When dad found out he did not want to talk about it. Mom wanted to shoot the sitter. I remembered overhearing a lot of arguments. In the end, the sitter was no longer welcome in our life. My family never spoke about the situation again. I never received counseling, and no one asked how I felt. I buried the memory within me, or so I thought. It was like the incident never happened, until I got married.

Sex with my first husband was nothing worth remembering. I just laid there. I did not move or participate. I didn't know what to do. Each time we had sex, all I ruminated about was the sitter on top of me. I thought that laying there was the way sex was supposed to be done. Those negative feelings from my childhood came back, and I just wanted them to end. The story I kept telling myself in my head was that sex was bad, and that I was bad at it. There was no enjoyment or pleasure for my husband or me.

After the divorce, I decided that I wanted to understand more about sex, so, I used each sexual experience after my divorce as a way to experiment. I was an engineer, and engineers use logic to solve a problem. If I tried this technique, did my partner like it or not? I used their reactions to decide if I was successful. No one ever asked me if I liked the sex, so how could I ask them? I started to understand what I liked and what I did not like, but I could never talk about it.

When I went to church, I was constantly bombarded with the notion that you were a sinner if you had sex outside of marriage. Sex was sinful for the unmarried woman. At church, they read the scripture that said the marital bed should be undefiled. What did that mean? Married people never discussed what went on behind the closed doors of the bedroom. No one would talk about sex!

In my mind, I decided that sex was something I could do without and that I was terrible at it. No one could convince me otherwise. I had suppressed talking about sex for so long, I did not even know how to bring the subject up.

Stephen was the first person with whom I could talk openly about what I liked. For the first time, I felt comfortable enough to talk about sex. When we were dating, we read a book of questions to find out more about each other. We each selected a question, and the other person had to answer honestly. There were many questions about sex. I purposefully asked Stephen these questions so I could understand how he thought about the topic. Then he started asking me the questions about sex. OMG! I gave him a simple yes or no at first, but as he shared openly with me, I began to share openly with him. I even told him about the sitter. Talking about sex before we got married allowed me to give to him my mind and my body.

I know that I am the perfect one for my husband. I know that he loves what I do, when I do it, and as much as I can do to satisfy his sexual desires. My confidence comes across as true love, and that love is what he wants from me. That unconditional love is true BLISS.

After being molested, what I know now is that talking about the incident and how it made me feel was the best way to heal my mind and emotions. Burying this inside me impacted my sex life. If I had talked about the event with someone, I might have understood earlier in my life how it did affect me. In many families and cultures, we hide bad emotions and situations and never talk about them. Suppressing those feelings eats us from the inside out. When we block out negative experiences, we adopt a protective behavior that does not allow us to talk about the subject. Later in life, this blockage prevents us from fully enjoying life and sexual relationships. The emotional pain shows up as a flinch when someone touches us. It shows on our face when the topic of our hurt is used in a joke. When we argue, we say things like, "You don't understand!"

If something terrible has happened to you, the only way to truly overcome it is to talk about it until you have fully released the emotion. Find a safe place to expose your inner thoughts. Discover a way to share your past to receive the healing you need. Whether you choose a professional, a friend, a journal, or a family member, talk about your experience when you are ready to heal. But the sooner you take this step, the faster you can heal. This openness will help you to begin to TALK STRAIGHT to yourself when you think about sex. Start now.

Stephen told me of a time when he went to a Philly cheese steak place in Philadelphia on South Street. There was a line zig-zagging, back and forth, in the store and out the door. The line moved quickly because of the restaurant's system. The woman in front of him started telling the grill man that she did not want onions, peppers, or mushrooms. He barked back at her, "Tell me what you do want, not what you don't want!" We should address our sexual wants and desires the same way. Tell your partner what you want. If I say, "I don't like it when you touch me like that," that statement may be true, but how *do* you want to be touched? If I say instead, "I love it when you touch me that way," then my partner knows exactly what I like and will do it more when they want to please me.

The thoughts in our head became the rules we played by when it came to sex. If we thought oral sex was nasty or that church girls never had oral sex, you never tried oral sex or felt bad if you did. You need to ask yourself, "What rules do I have about sex? Where did they come from? What if those rules are just simply not true?" I am not telling you to change your beliefs. What I am asking you to do is challenge them. If your principles remain true for you, then keep them. There is no right or wrong for you. If your partner feels the same way, then they may be the person for you. If your partner does not feel the same way, then try to understand why.

Own your sexual identity. If missionary sex is what you want, then be happy with it. If you want new experiences, then you must try something different. But before you try something new, you must change the way you look at it. As we stated in the previous chapters, you attract the outcome you think about. If you believe being on top is slutty, then when you try being on top you feel slutty. If you learn to TALK STRAIGHT about being on top and believe that it could be enjoyable for you and your partner, then your outcome will be more pleasurable.

To change the way you think about sex, you must receive new information. You need to do your research. For example, if I want to change the way I look, there

85

are many ways I can figure out what I want to look like. I could go to a cosmetic surgeon. I could go to the beauty store to buy new make-up. I could get a new hair style or change my clothing. I could copy the style of a movie star I liked. Do the same thing with sex. Pick up a book, use the internet, call an expert, talk to a friend, watch a movie, and more importantly, talk to your partner. If you don't know what to talk about, pick up a book about sex. Let the topics in the book lead your discussion. A book can help you break your limiting beliefs about sex, so you can reach nirvana and achieve BLISS.

It can be fun finding out what you like with your partner, but you must create a safe space to talk about sex with each other, without judgment. When Stephen and I were dating and vacationed in Denver, CO, we decided to go to an adult superstore together. This place was like a large department store of SEX. There were departments for everything; costumes, toys, movies, books, and furniture. Several products had a monitor above them showing their proper use. The sales staff was extremely helpful and explained the products we had questions about. This memory provides a lot of laughs thinking back on our experience in toy land. The best way to figure out what you like is by trial and error.

I recently hosted a couple's adult toy party. We invited married couples and single friends who were dating. The men heard from the other women ideals that improved their pleasure, while the women heard what the other men thought. We laughed so much that night, but I can say that each couple left better off than they came, and they bought a lot of toys that night. Until you know what you like or don't like, no one else will know what you want. Take your time. This process is not a race to get all your answers about sex in one night.

Stephen

Corn Starch

While we were dating, my wife and I decided to go to the Wisconsin Dells. It was going to be the most romantic weekend of my dating career. We had free tickets to see Roberta Flack at the casino. We also planned golfing, shopping, and horseback riding. This date was a mixture of activities we both liked. We decided to stay overnight at a bed and breakfast, in a room with a Jacuzzi next to the bed. We packed for the weekend, and brought wine, whipped cream, sexy lingerie, candles, candies, and fruit. We had a romantic walk down the main street and enjoyed a wonderful dinner. As night fell, we prepared for the night of our lives. There were no time limits and no limits on the number of times or what we could do.

I read an article that mentioned corn starch was a way to make your body feel silky during sex. So, we brought along a plastic drop cloth to lay over the bed and a big box of corn starch. We lit candles all over the room. We sprinkled the corn starch over the plastic and began to apply it to each other's bodies. At first, the powder made my skin feel silky, but then it began to get slippery. As we began to sweat, the corn starch created a huge mess. We looked like someone exploded a box of flour all over our two black bodies.

Corn starch did not do anything to enhance our sexual pleasure. We sat and laughed for a while at ourselves under the candlelight, sipping wine in the Jacuzzi. Although the experiment with corn starch did not go well, we have one of the best memories of going outside of our comfort zone with sex. Whenever we want a good laugh, we retell this story. Since that night, corn starch has never crossed our bedroom door again.

Sonji

The thoughts in my head today are positive, and I am no longer afraid to suggest to my husband something new, or to even boast about how good I have become. When I TALK STRAIGHT to myself about sex, I feel like no one is better than I am at pleasing my husband and that we will be forever in love and enjoying sex. Now that is sexy!

Sometimes what we learned about relationships comes from watching other examples of marriage; from our parents, our relatives, our neighbors, and our friends. We have positive and negative examples around us every day. We decide what to do in our relationships based upon the examples we have in front of us.

Sonji

The Submissive Wife

My parents have been married for over 50 years. When I was younger, I saw my mother take charge of the household and make all the financial decisions. She was a very strong and determined woman who, for the most part, got what she wanted. My father was very accommodating and tried to avoid conflict, so he let her have her way. In college, I decided that when I got married, I was going to be a submissive wife and let my future husband lead our family as I learned in Bible study. What I know now is that I did not truly understand being submissive or what marriage would be like.

I met my first husband during my freshmen year of college, and we dated exclusively. He was two years ahead of me in school. So, after he graduated, we began to drift apart. I did not want to believe that I had wasted my time falling in love, so I rejected the thought that we would not be together. At this point in my life, I was always successful in what I wanted, and I knew he was what I wanted. After I graduated, I moved from Ohio to Pennsylvania to be closer to him. Unfortunately, we were still 90 minutes away from each other. Here we were, in our twenties, with our whole life ahead of us, yet we never talked about our dreams.

After our five-year engagement period, I planned a wedding in my hometown of Mansfield, Ohio. The night before the wedding, he drove to his bachelor party an hour away. I remember being worried about whether he was going to come back and show up for the wedding. He called and asked me a few strange questions, which was enough to make me worry. I should have told him when he called, "If you feel that way, then we should not get married." But everyone was coming, and I could not bear to hear my mother tell me, "I told you so," or the embarrassment of being left at the altar.

I had no idea that if your fiancé is unsure about marrying you, then you should just call off the wedding or wait until they are sure. All I believed was if you loved someone, you should get married. I did not understand what it meant for someone to love me back. My parents had arguments, and my friends' parents had arguments, so that was what love looked like to me. If I had a disagreement with my fiancé, I thought arguments were just a part of love; there was no reason to call the wedding off. So, I married him.

91

After our wedding, I remembered that I planned to be a submissive wife. I never talked about it with him. I agreed with everything he wanted to do because that is what I thought a submissive wife did. I lost myself. I was no longer the vibrant, young woman with so much to offer, like when we were dating. If he asked me, "Where do you want to go to dinner?" I said, "I don't know. Wherever you want to go." Either we would go where he wanted, or we did not go out. I could see his disappointment, but I thought that if I kept this "submissive thing" up, he would see that I truly cared about what he wanted. Unfortunately, I had changed so much that I was no longer the person he fell in love with back in college.

Our marriage wasn't terrible, but it was not what either of us really wanted. We just went through the motions of how we thought a married couple should act. Although ours was not an abusive union, I still would not wish this type of relationship on anyone. My beliefs and the conversation in my head that I failed eroded my self-worth and confidence.

The best part about our marriage was the birth of our two children. We are friends, not just because of the children, but because we realized that our marriage was not what either of us needed. So why argue, fuss, or fight about it? We chose to just learn from the situation and move on. He has been married now for more than 22 years, and I am happy for him and his wife.

I learned so much from my first marriage, and I have applied those lessons to my second marriage. We talk and communicate every day. Stephen is truly my best friend. No one knows me better. We share our hopes and dreams, our likes and dislikes, and our past pains and joys. Sharing your dreams and thoughts is like sharing your inner soul. This intimacy is a great gift that someone offers to you. That belief is why some people are so hurt or betrayed when their partner shares their inner thoughts with someone else and not with them. Imagine how you would feel if your partner gave his or her wedding ring away. The wedding ring is a valuable, precious gift, right? To give it away would be unforgivable. Sharing your dreams and hopes is also a precious gift for many people. We only share such personal information with someone that we feel we can trust. If you don't feel you can share your hopes and dreams, why is that?

After I tried to become my idea of a submissive wife, the story in my head was that I failed at my first marriage. The thoughts in my head screamed that I was terrible at marriage. What I know now is that this assertion is an awful thing to tell yourself. So, now I TALK STRAIGHT by saying that my first marriage was a learning experience. That relationship was successful at teaching me what not to do in my next relationship. Throughout our lives people come and go; they move on and we move on. The Bible says that there is a season for everything under the sun. People have a season in your life. Your teachers come and go; your friends come and go. Even your family members may come and go. We don't think when one friend moves away that we are terrible at friendship. If we have a failing out, we don't say to ourselves, we will never have a friend again. We get up and make a new friend. So, I learned to leverage my first marriage as preparation for my second marriage. I no longer carry negative feelings about that relationship. We parted ways so that we can continue to live our lives in a more productive manner.

This process is how I started to TALK STRAIGHT about divorce.

What are you telling yourself about your marriage or relationships? Are the statements in your head positive or negative? Do they start out with loving statements but turn into mostly negative ones? If you can't say one positive word about the person you are with, then why are you with them? I am not telling you to leave someone, but can you turn those negative thoughts into positive ones? Make a bold decision to be positive! Look for the positive, not the negative.

My relationship with Stephen is about sharing, discussing, and coming to an agreement when decisions need to be made. When we can't agree, I recognize Stephen has our best interest at heart because he knows what we want to accomplish. I can trust that he will make the final decision and take 100% responsibility for its outcome because he considers what I think deeply. I do not get upset because I know he made the best decision he could, with the information he had. This is what I believe submission truly means today. This acceptance is how I TALK STRAIGHT about our marriage. I never dreamed I could have a relationship

95

like ours. Stephen and I are proud to be an example to so many people. Stephen has been married four times. Believe me, he has a lot of life lessons he leverages in our marriage today. I am so glad he did not give up on finding someone to love and appreciate him. You must pick and choose from our suggestions what you think could improve your relationship, as well as examples in your own life. The key is to know what you want in your life.

TALK STRAIGHT to your partner. We all know that the world can be a cruel place. Pillow talk is not just about the bedroom, it is about your conversations anytime and anywhere. Make your relationship a safe place to share thoughts, any time of day. Once someone shares their thoughts with you, use that intimacy to encourage and build them up. Do not tear them down or demean them. Use those thoughts to show how much you care because you heard them.

Each day when Stephen comes home, he is so excited to tell me about his day. I am also excited to share my day as well. Sometimes he can't wait until he gets home, so he calls me in the middle of the day. He wants to be free to share his every thought when they happen. Most of us need to vent so that we can get past the hurt and the frustration the world gives to us.

Sharing is about being heard and returning the favor. Some people don't share because they think they will be judged by the person listening. How many times when you were a kid did you keep a secret from your parents because you thought they were not going to like what you did? This programming continues into our adult life. Many people do not like to talk about their feelings, dreams, or thoughts because they may have been taught not to share, or bad things happened in the past when they did share. Maybe they shared their dreams with someone who made fun of them. Whatever the reason, know that to cultivate a relationship of communication, it will take time, a lot of practice, and learning new skills.

How do you make a safe place? You must be willing to take the first step and share your thoughts, feelings, and dreams with your partner. You must be a good listener. I like the Golden Rule, "Do unto others as you would like them to do unto you." If you want someone to listen to you, you must listen to them. There are many books and techniques on how to actively listen to someone if you want to become a good listener. What does a safe place look like? A safe place is anywhere you feel comfortable to talk and/or cry without judgment.

Most mornings before we leave the bed, Stephen and I pause and have a conversation. During the week, the exchange is brief, but still meaningful. On the weekends, our conversations are so much more in-depth. These conversations are the air that I need to start my day. We talk about what we dreamed about (if we can remember), what lessons we learned the previous day, what we want to accomplish this day, and how we feel about each other and our lives. We always find something to say.

Sonji and Stephen

Good morning, Sweetheart

A typical morning conversation for us goes like this:

Stephen: Good morning, Sweetheart. How did you sleep?

Sonji: I slept well. I didn't realize how tired I was. How long have you been awake?

Stephen: I've been up since 4 a.m. I went downstairs and did some writing and my yoga. I feel great. My life is wonderful!

Sonji: So many amazing things happen each day.

Stephen: Such as?

Sonji: Well yesterday I went to Zuppa's for lunch, and I was just standing for a few minutes, waiting patiently. I saw that the workers were doing something, so I just waited. They came over after a minute or two. When I got to the register the woman said, "I am going to give you a free dessert since you so patiently waited for us." I know little stuff like that happens to us all the time, but I am always so amazed.

Stephen: Yes, it is the result of being positive and the Law of Attraction. People are attracted to our positive natures.

Sonji: Thanks for understanding I was so tired last night. I am so thankful for having you in my life. You are an amazing husband. I've got plenty of time and strength now!

Stephen: Oh yeah! You are so welcome. You deserve it. Thanks for always keeping your word. Now get over here!

Sonji

You may think, "How mushy is that? People don't talk that way." Well, I am here to tell you, we do talk like that whenever we get the chance. How much better would your day go if you started it off talking kindly to your partner? We had to practice.

TALK STRAIGHT about how you feel. Don't play games. If you love someone then say it! My mother often said, "Well, he should know that I love him." NO! Say it! Then there will not be any confusion. Say it daily. Speaking about love doesn't have to be a big production. In the morning when I wake, I say "I love you." Before I go to bed at night, I say "I love you." Stephen does not have to guess how I feel about him.

Tell your partner why you are in love with them. It is so powerful to hear why someone loves you. When you tell someone why you love them, you reinforce the good behaviors you appreciate. I read books about raising kids that stated that you should tell your children what to do, not what they shouldn't do. If you tell a child what not to do, then he or she must guess what to do. If you tell them what to do then they know their purpose, and they know you like their actions. When expressing love to someone, which way is better?

Option 1: Honey, I love you because you take care of me. You make sure I eat. You help me remember when I forget.

Option 2: Honey, I love you because you don't leave your clothes around the house. I love you because you don't fuss at me when I forget stuff.

I am sure you will agree that Option 1 is a better way to tell someone what you want them to keep doing. Option 1 tells them that you like it when they take care of you, cook for you, and remind you. So, if they love you, they will continue to do these things. Option 2 tells them what you don't like but not what you do like. The Option 2 person is left to guess what they need to do to please you.

Communication between you and your partner is critical to a successful relationship True communication determines whether you will be in alignment with each other or slowly drifting apart, but you already know that reality. Through my conversations with Stephen, I have learned that sex to his body is like the air he needs to breathe. Men need to release tension in their bodies. Just like a crabby girl friend, who has not had sex in a while, we joke and say, "You need to get laid." Men are similar; if he doesn't release with me, eventually he will need a way to release. Recognizing that having sex is important to his well-being allows me to see sex in a unique way. If his body needed a certain medication to improve his quality of life, I would do everything I could to get it for him. That is how I TALK STRAIGHT about giving my husband the sex he needs. Because I believe this fact, and I deliver, he does what is in his power to do the same for me.

We have covered a lot in this chapter, so let's take time to summarize. Saying positive things to yourself and to your partner about sex is important. Communicate what you do want, as opposed to what you don't want. Be equally yoked in sex and relationships by being clear on your expectations. You must have a positive environment with a safe place to have pillow talk in order to achieve true communication. TALK STRAIGHT about sex takes practice, practice, practice, in more ways than one, if you know what I mean.

CHAPTER FIVE

COULDA, WOULDA, SHOULDA

How to Release Regret

Stephen

As we wrote this book, I realized that one thing that hinders our ability to TALK STRAIGHT is regret. When people have regret, they say things like: "I should be further along in life than I am;" "I should have amassed more wealth;" "My life would have been different if I had not spent so much time in that relationship;" "If I had not dropped out of college, I could have started my own business." There are so many things that we choose to regret. We will call this the land of Coulda, Woulda, Shoulda (CWS). CWS was inspired by a song written by the late great, Lou Rawls. We have all been to the land of CWS. "I should have gotten that job, so I could have made more money, and I would be able to get my head above water." Let's face it, we are human. The problem comes when we stay in CWS-Land too long. Even if you TALK STRAIGHT, but you have regret about the topics you want to resolve, the positive and powerful words you say will not produce the maximum results.

Sonji

The Door

My son was 12-years-old and just returned for the summer when I met Stephen. My son lived with his father in the Boston area for his 6th grade year. He was a typical pre-teen boy who wanted to play video games every chance he got. He had lots of friends and was smart, but he acted out by not performing up to his abilities in school. I am not sure, but I think his acting out had to do with his relationship with his father and me. My son's father and I decided that it was good for my son to move back with me for his 7th grade year. Stephen and I were recently married and together we discussed with my son what would happen if he failed to do his school work and chores.

On one day, after repeatedly failing to do what he was told, the consequences were administered. Stephen removed the door to my son's room. All I remembered after that incident was that my son decided he wanted to live with his father from then on. I did not fight his decision. I knew making such a decision was difficult for him, and I did not want to add any more pain or pressure to his situation. But secretly, I blamed Stephen for my son's decision to go live with his father and not live with me anymore. Over time, I regretted letting my baby boy go. I called routinely, and he visited me on the holidays and during the summer. But I felt I had lost him forever. I should have intervened and stopped Stephen from taking the door down. We should not have been so hard on my son; after all, he was only a typical boy. I feel that in some way the removal of that door, also removed my ability to discipline our other children together with Stephen. The regret I felt over my son subconsciously affected my decisions on how to interact with our other children. I was afraid that if I was too harsh, our daughters might leave like my son did. I did not want Stephen to experience the pain I had from losing my son. Although I know Stephen did what he thought was best to make sure my son was respectful, I still could not help but miss my boy.

The next time my son lived with me was after he finished his freshman year in college. He was so depressed; from what, I did not really understand. My regret resurfaced. I thought, "If only I had fought for him, he would have lived with me and dealt with life much better." I cried from the pain of watching my son struggle with his depression and trying to find his new direction. Now that he was an adult, my son and I needed to develop a new relationship. We talked, argued, and discussed how we felt. Dealing with an adult son was really hard. I finally understood and appreciated the strength that Stephen exhibited throughout this tough time. I forgave myself for holding on to regret for so long.

But what really helped me was when I called my son before I wrote this story and talked about the incident with the door. He told me, "I am alright, mom. I am glad you allowed me to make my own decision without adding pressure." Knowing how he feels today helps me to heal the pain caused by regret. Giving a voice to my regret with those involved allowed me to release it. I have a relationship today with my son and with Stephen without any regret.

Stephen

How many times as parents, do we wish we taught our child something that could have altered their course in life? How many times do we regret that we did not give them enough of what we believe they needed back then? We have stated several times in this book that our parents did the best they could with the information they had at the time. Those of us who are parents need to recognize that the same principle applies to us. We have done and are doing the best we can with the information available to us now. With this statement we can start to let go of regret.

Regret shows up in many ways. We all, at one point or another, have had regret, yet it looks different for each and every one of us. For some, regret is a thought of remorse that you get over quickly by acknowledging it and moving on. Other people deal with regret for many years or even a lifetime. For example, you might feel like you wasted your time going to college because you can't find a job, or the job you have can't pay off the loans you accumulated. You may think, "I should have studied something else," or that your career is going nowhere, with no chance of advancement. Instead of letting go of regret and selecting a new job or going back to school to study something different, we hold on to regret and stay in our miserable job for 20 years. You may be in a very unhappy relationship today, regretting the one you let go. Rather than leaving this unhappy relationship, you stay out of the fear of making another wrong decision. In each example, you are living in CWS land, allowing a single regret to affect the rest of your life.

No matter the duration of your regret, the process to deal with it is the same. We have included several tips on how to get rid of regret, but some are going to need more help than others to let go. Regret can be so deep and ingrained in the fabric of your being that you may need help from a professional. I want you to know, whatever you do to get rid of regret will be worth the effort! You must find the right combination of actions that work for you. How much help you are willing to get and how fast you want to rid yourself of regret will depend on how desperately you want to live a life of BLISS.

When regret becomes a part of a person's life, it causes them to stagnate and ruminate, and deeply affects their behavior. If your regret involves a family member, you might stop talking to them for years. You could be angry around them. You might say disrespectful comments or pick fights. Why do we hold on to regret, sometimes for years? Because we hope that the other person will recognize how they wronged us and maybe, one day, apologize. Don't wait for an apology. When you wait for the other person to behave in a certain way, you give them control of your life. You give yourself permission to stagnate and wait on them to show remorse. Too many people live in this type of regret: "If only they would come back and apologize. One day they are going to see the errors of their ways." No, they will not make an apology, and if they do see the error of their ways, they might not even tell you about it. Stop waiting on others. Do what you need to do, and just be happy with the results.

Regret causes you to look at what could have been instead of recognizing what is and what can be. If you want to have a life of BLISS, you have got to stop looking back, feeling sorry for yourself, or wishing you made better choices. Sure, you could have chosen differently, but you didn't. So what? I have had many opportunities to live in regret: I have been divorced three times; I dropped out of high school; I was kicked out of the army. I could have looked at what was going on in my life and said, I should have done this, that, and a third. My wife said to me recently, "If anyone has a reason to regret, surely you do!"

As you may recall earlier in the book, I was raised by a mom that suffered from mental illness called schizoaffective disorder. We went through a lot of instability and volatile situations with her that were devastating. My childhood was always up and down, and I could have said, "What if my mom wasn't sick?" My dad was very seldom in my life growing up, and I could have said, "If only my dad was there, I would not have done this, or I could have learned that." This type of regret is about regretting the circumstances I found myself in. We romanticize what life could be like if only circumstances were different. But I want you to know, life is what it is, and we may not have control over many situations, but we can decide today what our life will be.

We develop regret when we try to keep score and we feel like we got short-changed. Maybe you were in a relationship and you felt like you gave your all but did not get much of anything in return. This type of regret is an example of keeping score. You compare what you put into the relationship against your view of what someone else should have placed into it. You formed a belief from watching what you thought was a good marriage. When you meet that someone special, your relationship meter starts recording. You start measuring how much they do according to the standard in your head. Over time, if they fail to reach your standards, then you start to regret that you wasted time with someone who didn't love you in the manner you thought you deserved. The story in your head about what it takes to have a good relationship, paints you as the victim in your story. Your mind will never paint you as the evil one, or as being in the wrong. Therefore, you view every situation as if you got the short end of the stick (a stick you created), and now you live in regret.

For some people, living in regret takes the blame for your life off you and places it somewhere else. "No one will give me a job because I don't have GED." "No one told me that getting a career in this field would not give me the means to live the life I wanted." "Because my spouse cheated on me, I can't trust anyone anymore." Stop giving your power away! Get a GED today. Find a new career. Get help on how to trust again. Many people have been where you are and now live a life of BLISS because they stopped living in regret.

I have a good friend who told me that he should be further along in life. Many people feel the same way. Whenever you use the word 'should,' you put the responsibility for the outcomes of your life in someone else's hands. You are saying, if they do 'this,' then I should be able to do 'that.' This belief ties your outcome to their actions. 'Should' also implies that this action is what normal people do. 'Should' is a scapegoat or a relief valve that lets you off the hook. Using 'should' allows you to take less than 100% responsibility for the results you produce. Understand that you are in your present situation because of the thoughts you had, the words you spoke, and the actions you took throughout your life.

What does it mean to accept 100% responsibility? It means to stop blaming others for your current circumstances. Some of you might say, "I did not blame anyone," because you did not use their name directly. But you did blame them by using 'should.'

When you use the word 'should,' ask yourself, "Who should have done what?" Then you will know who you are blaming. To take responsibility, take out the word 'should' and rephrase the sentence, identifying the role you played in getting you to your current situation.

TALK STRAIGHT Examples for Dealing with Regret		
Blaming Statement	**What You are Really Saying**	**100% Accountable**
I should have gotten that job	The hiring manager should have given the job to me	I will be more prepared next time
I should not have married him/her	I should have married someone else or; I should not have gotten married at all	I chose you and I will make the best of this relationship or move on
He cheated on me	He did me wrong	I need to know how I contributed to a relationship that does not serve me and take an appropriate action that serves my needs

TALK STRAIGHT Examples for Dealing with Regret		
Blaming Statement	**What You are Really Saying**	**100% Accountable**
They should have valued me more	They don't see all the hard work I put into this job	I will do a better job of expressing and documenting my value. I know my worth
I should have studied something else in school	I can't make enough money in this field	I must be more creative in generating income

We all develop habits of regret. Sometimes our remorse is easy to recognize, and other times it is not. When I say the same negative statement over and over, I create a habit of regret. If every time I take a test I say, "I passed that test, but I should have studied harder," I create a habit of regret. If after every performance review at work, I say, "I got a raise, but I should have gotten more," I create a habit of regret. Regret is never being fully happy with the present or the past. Regret can really work us over; it robs us of our present and our future. When I focus on what happened to me in the past, it distracts me from being fully present; it stops me from being thankful and grateful. Regret is a thief that robs you of your BLISS and takes you out of your place of peace. Regret places your focus so much in the past, you miss the present. Whatever happened in the past or didn't occur the way we wanted it to, let it go. Sometimes we feel a need to try to go back and fix what went wrong. You must teach yourself to believe the best is yet to come and to be thankful for where you are now. If you want to have BLISS, you cannot live in the past. Do what you can now. Take inspired action. Be the best you can be.

Sonji

You must address regret, so that your words, thoughts, and actions are aligned and moving in the same direction. As Lisa Nichols says, "The tongue in your mouth and the tongue in your shoe need to move in the same direction." This means that it is hard to move forward if you are looking back. When words are not aligned, you send two different messages into the universe. "I want to start a business, but I don't believe I can do it because I should have..." Whichever of the two opposing thoughts you believe in more will guide your actions and direction. You will self-sabotage subconsciously, or perhaps consciously, if the regret is stronger than the future direction. Imagine how much power you would have without your baggage of regret? If you can truly let go of regret, then everything you believe and say will work together and drive faster results toward your BLISS. Your new message will become, "I can use my degree and what I learned on my job to run my own business." Finally, you are in alignment with your words and thoughts!

Stephen

As long as, you hold on to the hurt, anger, and disappointment of the past, they will rob you of experiencing real BLISS. Once I was able to forgive myself and others, I was able to release the regret. This journey is a process, and we are continually growing and learning. Every time you let go and forgive, your life gets a little bit better. BLISS is your birthright; forgiveness and gratitude are the path to get you to your BLISS. Forgiveness is not for the person who wronged you. You are not giving them permission to hurt you again. Forgiveness means you release yourself from the pain. You release yourself from the event. You release your life to a future where you have no regrets and begin to TALK STRAIGHT to yourself.

CHAPTER SIX

LOVE THE ONE
YOU'RE WITH

Stephen

Our concluding chapter is about how to show love to the person you are with the most: YOU! You may be wondering, what does it mean to love oneself, what does this self-love look like, how will I know if I am doing it right, or will I recognize BLISS when it shows up? The answers to these questions are different for everyone, but the answers lie within you. You are the expert on you. In order to 'love the one you are with,' you must be kind to yourself first.

We sometimes are too hard on ourselves. Take time to celebrate you and your accomplishments. Remind yourself about the good that you have done. Recognize the effort you put forth. Let yourself off the hook, and don't punish yourself for past mistakes or indiscretions. You are still worthy of love. When we were kids, we use to yell, "Do over," when things did not turn out as we wanted. So, use that childlike spirit that you have buried deep down inside, and yell, "Do over!" If you want BLISS in your life, you must give BLISS. Remember, our definition of BLISS involves complete forgiveness without any judgment. You must forgive yourself, without any judgment, to show yourself love.

The next thing you must do is believe your life will get better. My therapist encouraged me to keep a journal and write about the chaos and confusion in my life. I continued to write, no matter how depressing the story got. I had to tell myself that life wasn't over and that it would get better, even when life did not look or feel like it could possibly improve. Even when I could not see any physical signs of improvement, I had to believe life would get better. Then, I was laid off from my job. I could have chosen to ruminate about how terrible life was all day, or I could make a bold decision to do better, live better, and be better. I had to learn to love me, the right way, for who I was, in that moment. This endeavor was not easy. I was in the middle of my third divorce, and I became depressed as I went through financial hardship, as well. I had to look back at my journal and remember the difficulties I had already been though and recognize how I made it through those hardships. No matter how awful the circumstances seemed to me at the current time, I was glad that I had made it through other similar situations. I was okay. I used every tool I could think of to help me through this low point in my life. There was an old church song that said, "I don't believe he brought me this far to leave me." Those words helped me to TALK STRAIGHT when I could not think of anything better or more specific to say. Singers and song-writers give us words to say when we can't express our feelings. Find a few songs that inspire you with positive words to help you TALK STRAIGHT.

Before I could love me, I had to like me; I had to build up to loving me. The little things that friends did for me provided encouragement. When someone gives of themselves to you, it sparks a bit of hope in you that you are worthy of kindness and good things happening in your life. A friend of mine named Sherrell came over, and we played Scrabble. This quality time with my friend nourished me because it made me forget my

121

current circumstances and showed me that if I could be happy for one hour, maybe I could be happy for an entire day or even a whole week, and so on. Find a positive influence to spend time with, or a way to nourish your soul. Find or create positive affirmations and say them aloud every day. Be thankful for where you are today. All your experiences play a part in making you a better person, even the difficult ones, which Lisa Nichols describes as, "a gift wrapped in sand paper." Learn to appreciate all the gifts you receive.

It does not matter how many times you fall. You need to celebrate every time you get back up. You did not give up. You did not become so discouraged or depressed that you ended your life. When you were a child, you learned how to walk. How many times did you fall? You did not become discouraged or depressed. You did not give up on walking. You did not say, "I am just going to forget this walking thing and crawl or roll wherever I need to go." You kept on trying. You had people around you to cheer you on and celebrate every baby step you took until you were a pro. You need to be as resilient today as you were then! You need people around you who will celebrate your baby steps. Can you imagine what your life would look like if you were celebrated for everything you tried? Well, start celebrating with YOU.

Be the positive light that you need. Life boils down to the choices we make or those we fail to take. One of the most profound lessons I learned was an equation, E+R=O. Events plus Responses equals Outcomes. The event is a situation that happens. Some events we have control over, but many we do not. By controlling our responses, we can influence the outcome. We can't control the outcome, but we can help the outcome be in our favor if we choose positive responses. Everything that happens in our lives can be used to produce positive outcomes. If you learn from all events, then you can produce new outcomes you want by responding favorably.

How you respond can get you closer to the outcome you desire. We all are faced with obstacles and challenges. Your response makes all the difference in the world. How you view the event often determines how you will respond to it. There were times when I felt I could not do anything right. My response to every event was to feel upset or depressed. I chose to respond to each failure the same way. Repetition breeds expectation, so every time things did not work out, my response was to catastrophize about the situation which depressed me even more. But my negative response did not produce the outcome I wanted. When I learned about the E+R=O equation, I realized that I had a choice. So, rather than respond negatively, I chose a positive response. I chose to look for the positive in every situation. If you did not get the promotion you wanted, your old response might have been to stop going the extra mile, but your new response would be to appreciate the job you have and use your gifts and expertise to help those around you. If your child broke your favorite glass figurine, you could get upset and yell, or you could recognize that you love your child more than that item. I celebrated each time I responded positively. The more I responded positively, the easier making optimistic choices got. People around me started to celebrate with me. They wanted to contribute to my positive attitude, and even better positive events started happening. Celebrating small victories and successes will create positive thoughts and feelings and will give you enthusiasm and energy to try again and again. I have heard others refer to this as your bounce-back muscle. Like any muscle, you need to exercise it to strengthen it.

Sonji

Postal Money Order Bounce Back

Recently, I needed to get a visa for a business trip to Brazil. I spent three hours pulling all the documents together and applying for my visa on-line. Part of the process was to give the original documents to the Brazilian consulate. The process would go faster if I took the documents to them in person. I needed to have the visa back in 10 days if I were going to arrive when the location wanted me to be there. There was an office in Chicago which was an hour and a half from our home. I made plans to go the very next day.

My plan was to leave my home around 7:30 a.m., so I could be in Chicago when the office opened at 9 a.m. I don't know why, but the Consulate only accepted applications between 9 and 11 a.m. My calls that morning ran overtime. I bounced back from my late start by deciding not to worry because I would still arrive by 10 a.m. Construction was terrible along the highway, and I missed a turn, somehow ending up on

Lower Wacker Drive which runs underneath Chicago. I was worried that I would not know where to park. But I bounced back from my frustration of missing my exit and not knowing where to park by reassuring myself that I would still have plenty of time. Miraculously, when I finally found the address, I realized I was at the valet parking for the building I wanted.

I went upstairs to the office and noticed a sign which stopped me dead in my tracks. "We only accept postal money orders as payment. No cash, checks or credit cards." OMG! I forgot to think about how I was going to pay for the visa! Did I just waste my time coming down here? I could have just cried and turned around and left, but instead I bounced back from my fear of having wasted my time and reminded myself that I had the ability to figure this out. Because I didn't cuss or yell, two ladies waiting patiently for their turn offered their assistance. One woman offered to sell me an extra postal money order she had. Amazing, right? I asked the clerk how much I needed to pay for my visa. I needed $160, but the woman's money order was for only $120. Darn. The second woman explained that she got hers from a post office that was not far from our location and helped me find the address.

I shook off my disappointment at this major mistake, bounced back and decided to give all the effort I had to still turn this mistake around. I had one hour before the window closed. I decided to leave my car parked and take a taxi. The post office was six minutes away in Chicago traffic. When I arrived at the post office, I ran in. There were two people in line and two more already at the counter. I could have just given up right then. There was no way I would make it back in time. But I bounced back yet again, and nicely asked the people in line if I could go ahead of them to make it back to the office before closing. They agreed. Another blessing! The people at the counter still took a long time. Finally, after 15 minutes of waiting, I was able to get the money order. Because I asked the others if I could move ahead in line, I was able to make it back to the office with 10 minutes to spare, which was another miracle.

With my money order in hand and happy that I had overcome all these obstacles, I waited and then approached the clerk. Everything was in order, except one more detail I missed. I had the wrong letter signed! I had a letter from my visiting office and not the one from my home office which I needed. I was not able to get the visa, and again, I wanted to just cry. I could have thrown a tantrum or cussed the clerk out; I deserved to with the morning I just had. But instead of being upset, I asked a few clarifying questions so that I would not make the same mistake twice. I left the office feeling a little disappointed.

After all I went through that morning, how could the universe not allow me to turn in my visa application? Everything seemed to line up so perfectly. There were eight amazing circumstances working in my favor. Nevertheless, I decided not to let this dilemma ruin my evening plans of celebrating my niece's birthday. Because I TALKED STRAIGHT to myself and used my bounce-back muscle, I did not get arrested, and I had a great weekend. To celebrate, I posted live on Facebook about this story and received many comments from my friends and family who were proud of me for using my bounce-back muscle.

Stephen

The bounce-back muscle is inside of all of us. Reading this book is a terrific way to help build your bounce-back muscle. This muscle may be a little dormant because you have not used it much lately, but it is there inside you. Recent events and negative thought patterns might overshadow your inner strength, but once you realize you allowed negativity to creep into your life, you can bounce back to the positive. When you TALK STRAIGHT and change your negative thoughts into positive ones you are using your bounce-back muscle. You can bounce back to having BLISS. Bounce back to the freedom to love and be loved in abundance, with complete forgiveness, and without judgment.

I am thankful today for my job. This job has at times pressed, stretched, pulled, and almost crushed me and my spirit. Yet those experiences at my job gave me the desire to write this book and to start a business that helps others push past adverse circumstances. Today, I have a very happy and successful family. I have been very happily married for 10 years. We have a blended family with five kids who are well-adjusted, young

129

adults, ranging from 19 to 24 years old. My family life today is completely different from how I grew up.

I have nine siblings due to all of my mother's husbands and all my daddy's wives and girlfriends. My dad married three times, and mom was married four times. When I look at the four times I got married, I guess you could say the apple does not fall from the tree. But I like that old philosophy, if at first you don't succeed, try, try again. I could have given up on marriage after the second or third one, but my bounce back muscle was so strong, I just knew there was someone out there who would love me and support me for who I am.

For the first five years of my life, starting at five weeks of age, I grew up in my grandparent's home without either parent. Throughout my life, I witnessed, and in some instances experienced personally, physical and mental abuse, alcoholism, drug addiction, poverty, and infidelity. There was an endless rotation of step-parents, step-brothers and sisters, and half-brothers and sisters. I moved 10 times across four different states before I was 18 years old. There were times when we had plenty, and times we didn't. I know what it is like to be on welfare, to receive food stamps, to shop only at Goodwill for clothing and school supplies, and to receive Christmas presents from the Salvation Army delivery truck. I have lived in trailer homes, Section Eight housing, and nice houses in well-off neighborhoods. My mom even created her own religion and Bible during, what I call, the "Birds on a Wire" phase. All her decisions were made based upon whether the birds were sitting on the wire or not. If they were sitting on the wire, the answer to any question asked would be no. We could not even go to school if the birds were sitting on the wire. She suffered from mental illness, but I did not know that at the time. My mother even visited Jim Jones' church in California, before they moved to Guyana. Thank God, she did not like that church! If I can bounce back from all these events and more that happened in my life, then I am sure you can too. You can find these and many more stories about my life in my upcoming autobiography to be published soon.

I once heard that the true definition of forgiveness is not wishing the past was any different than it was. You are who you are today because of the sum of all your experiences. Rather than regret the events in your past, learn from them by asking yourself the right questions. Try not to repeat your mistakes, and most of all, TALK STRAIGHT about them. In doing so, you will show love to the one you are with and start to experience BLISS.

Throughout this book we described the B.L.I.S.S. process that we used to find our BLISS. I was BOLD in my decision to find a wife that supported and loved me after three divorces. Sonji LEVERAGED her previous two experiences of downsizing to not worry the third time, knowing things would work out either way. We provided examples of INSPIRED actions to deal with regret. By loving the one you are with, we showed you how to put yourSELF first. And now that you have finished this book, you can START now to TALK STRAIGHT on your road to BLISS.

We sincerely hope that this book has helped to move you forward on your life journey. Let us know how this book has helped you by leaving a comment on our website _www.MyBLISStopia.com_, posting your testimonial at _www.facebook.com/MyBLISStopia/_, or emailing us at Stephen@MilletEnterprises.com, and by sharing this book with others. At Millet Enterprise, we help you turn your negative thoughts into powerful actions and obstacles into opportunities, and your tragedies into triumphs to improve your life, find abundance, and experience BLISS. When you learn to TALK STRAIGHT DAMMIT about yourself, you will gain the capacity to live in BLISS, freedom, and love. May you be loved, have abundance, and find complete forgiveness without judgment. Namaste.

Appendix

TOOLS TO TALK STRAIGHT

Here are a few tips on how to TALK STRAIGHT to yourself and others. You need to figure out what works for you through trial and error. There is no magic combination that will work for everyone, all the time. Make a copy of this list to remind you.

1. Find an accountability partner who is positive or someone who is working to be positive. This person could be your spouse, your parents, or a friend. Having like-minded, positive people around you will accelerate your process.

2. Identify the negative people in your life and start reducing your exposure to them.

3. Create a list of affirmations. Write down the positive affirmations you want to say to yourself. Put them where you can see them several times a day. Say them every day. You can download our free affirmation list from our website: www.MyBLISStopia.com.

4. Make a play-list of positive music that uplifts you. Choose songs that describe your life positively and how you want it to be. Here are a few songs we love, if you can't think of any.

Suggested TALK STRAIGHT Playlist:

- "Ain't No Woman (Like the One I Got)" by Four Tops
- "This Will Be (an Everlasting Love)" by Natalie Cole
- "Dear Future Husband" by Meghan Trainor.
- "Bigger" by Sugarland
- "Real Good Man" by Tim McGraw
- "My, My, My" by Johnny Gill
- "This is How We Do It" by Montell Jordan
- "Sweet Love" by The Commodores
- "Let It Be" by The Beetles
- "We're a Winner" by The Impressions
- "Fly Like an Eagle" by Steve Miller Band
- "Enjoy Yourself" by The Jacksons
- "Imagine" by John Lennon
- "Happy" by Pharrell Willams

5. Join or create a community of people or a tribe that will support you and celebrate you.

6. Read self-help books. Here are books we read that helped us.

Books to Help You TALK STRAIGHT:

- *Abundance Now* by Lisa Nichols.
- *The Four Agreements* by Don Miguel Ruiz
- *The Fifth Agreement* by Don Miguel Ruiz
- *Wishes Fulfilled* by Wayne Dyer
- *The Success Principles* by Jack Canfield
- *You are a Bad Ass* by Jen Sincero

7. Forgive yourself. Sit in front of the mirror and talk to yourself like you would if you were forgiving someone else.

8. Love yourself. Say "I LOVE ME" everyday in the mirror. Do nice things for yourself.

9. Have an attitude of gratitude. Write down everything for which you are grateful. Keep in a journal, an app on your phone, or post it on your wall on big paper. Having it in your face every day helps you to remember them when times get tough.

10. Celebrate every small success and victory. Tell someone who will celebrate with you. Text them to a friend. Post them on Facebook. Write them down in your journal with your gratitudes, so that you can see your progress overtime.

Let us know how these tips have helped you by leaving a comment on our website www.MyBLISStopia.com, posting your testimonial at www.facebook.com/MyBLISStopia/, or emailing us at Stephen@MilletEnterprises.com, and by sharing our book TALK STRAIGHT DAMMIT with others.

49997770R00080

Made in the USA
Columbia, SC
30 January 2019